100 SOUTHERN ARTISTS

E. Ashley Rooney
With Paula Allen

Schiffer Publishing Ltd

4880 Lower Valley Road • Atglen, PA 19310

Acknowledgments

The creative act never ceases to amaze me; each new book is a novel experience, an adventure, and a challenge. There is a reason why I selected these artists for this book — their work is exciting; they look to the future; and I learn from them. Many galleries offered significant help: Barbara Archer Gallery, Chroma Art Gallery, Hughes Gallery, If ART Gallery, Marcia Wood Gallery, Principle Gallery, and Pryor Fine Art.

Paula Allen, whose work has been shown throughout the world, adds some phenomenal talent to this book. She certainly knows the South's artistic history and how to explain it to the layman. Finally, Barbara Purchia's dedicated proofreading is a godsend.

Other Schiffer Books by the Author:
100 Artists of the Midwest, 978-0-7643-4105-2, $45.00
100 Artists of New England, 978-0-7643-3665-2, $45.00
100 Artists of the Mid-Atlantic, 978-0-7643-3734-5, $45.00

Other Schiffer Books on Related Subjects:
100 Artists of the West Coast, 0-7643-1931-0, $39.95
100 Artists of the West Coast II, 978-0-7643-3271-5, $39.99
100 Artists of the Southwest, 0-7643-2414-4, $39.95

Cover and book designed by: Bruce Waters
Type set in Humanist 521 BT

ISBN: 978-0-7643-4241-7
Printed in China

Published by Schiffer Publishing, Ltd.
4880 Lower Valley Road
Atglen, PA 19310
Phone: (610) 593-1777; Fax: (610) 593-2002
E-mail: Info@schifferbooks.com

For the largest selection of fine reference books on this and related subjects, please visit our website at:
www.schifferbooks.com.
You may also write for a free catalog.

This book may be purchased from the publisher.
Please try your bookstore first.

We are always looking for people to write books on new and related subjects. If you have an idea for a book, please contact us at
proposals@schifferbooks.com

Schiffer Books are available at special discounts for bulk purchases for sales promotions or premiums. Special editions, including personalized covers, corporate imprints, and excerpts can be created in large quantities for special needs. For more information contact the publisher.

In Europe, Schiffer books are distributed by
Bushwood Books
6 Marksbury Ave.
Kew Gardens
Surrey TW9 4JF England
Phone: 44 (0) 20 8392 8585; Fax: 44 (0) 20 8392 9876
E-mail: info@bushwoodbooks.co.uk
Website: www.bushwoodbooks.co.uk

PHOTO CREDITS
COVER: Courtesy of Ashleigh Burke Coleman, Carol Gallagher, G. Frank Hart, Giovanni Lunardi Photography, Jan Clayton Pagratis, Jerry Siegel, Jess Elizabeth Handy, John Olsen, Patrick Tinkley Photography, Richard's Photography-Tallahassee, FL
BACK COVER: Gwenneth Barth-White, *The Orange Cutter* (André Longchamp Geneva); John Beard, *Portuguese Traffic Jam*; Patti Brady, *Rosalee's Rose* (Eli Warren); Sid Daniels, *Follies Twins*; Bill Farnsworth, *Racing Against the Storm*; Courtney Garrett, *Waiting in the Water, No. 5*; Dean Gioia, *Poseys Sunset 1985* (Richard's Photography-Tallahassee, FL); Geoffrey Johnson, *Study for Memorial* (Ali Ringenberg/Principle Gallery); Marcus Kenney, *The New Communism* (Imke Lass); Dale Kennington, *The Debutantes*; Marcello Novo, *Journey*; Morgan Santander, *Free Bird*; and Ebeth Scott-Sinclair, *Grandma's Bounty*.
SPINE: Peter Cerruta, *I'm Simply an Ordinary Lady*.

Contents

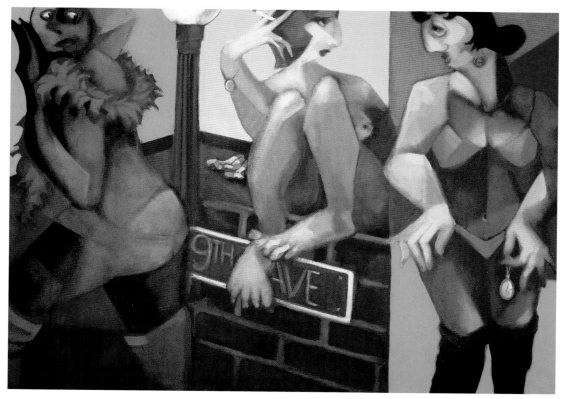

Peter Cerruta, *Ok, Ladies Let's Go. Time is Money.*

Foreword

Southern Art Transcends Boundaries

Paula Allen

My studies as an art student in the northeastern United States were mostly studies of European and New York artists. Very rarely did we ever study art of the southern United States. When I came to live and work in the South, I began to see more art directly influenced by nature, water, and sunlight. I started to meet artists who were directly working in versions of art forms I had never been exposed to before, such as print-making, textiles, ceramics, and painting. As a working southern artist since 1998, I've embraced the South and worked with other southern artists, side by side, to help bring southern art into the future.

The South has a rich tradition of storytelling, customs, language, and folklore. The stories of the region are featured in paintings in every century in traditional and nontraditional iconography. In these stories, the southern landscape plays a major role just as it does in southern art. While the scented sooth of the gardenias and magnolias waft into the canopy of live oaks and Spanish moss, they eternally hang over the ceiling of the South, setting the scene for centuries of history. Just as scent triggers a memory, these landscapes also influence and inspire artists to capture the rich traditions of the people of the South. Personally, I find that the southern landscape transformed my work into an expressionistic view of nature that I had not addressed when I lived in the Northeast.

Before the Nineteenth Century

Like the history of our nation, art in the South began with Native Americans. As an essential piece of everyday life, southeastern Native American cultures used and continue to use visual arts to communicate social systems and sacred traditions. Each tribe has their own ancient art traditions in tribal clothing, ceramics, sculptures, paintings, textiles, and beadwork. Nature and storytelling have always been prevalent subjects in Native American art and continue to be at the soul of southern art. Europeans who journeyed to the region to claim lands for their countries, found themselves fascinated by the Eden of possibilities they found. Artists like John James Audubon captured the beauty of South through his watercolors, which became vastly popular worldwide and sparked further interest in the region from other artists.

A sudden interest in colonizing the South led to a diverse community of Europeans consisting of French, German, English, and Spanish. European art traditions blended with southern nature landscapes to create a new genre of paintings. While portraiture remained the most popular style, these paintings were a blend of classical and romantic imagery and told the stories of the South through the lens of an observer. Immigrants also traveled to North Carolina and created red ware from the local clay. The ceramics traditions in North Carolina grew during this time and have continued to evolve for centuries. These crafts and fine arts conveyed the changing landscape of the untamed and untapped South.

Similar to eighteenth and nineteenth century dramatic literature, attitudes towards country versus city sophistication were apparent in city dwellers' perspectives toward the rural South. Many believed the South could not produce meaningful art because of its mainly rural and agrarian rooted culture. The region's distinct history in relation to its rural culture, however, is what made it intriguing for artists; European artists, such as Jeremiah Theus and Thomas Addison Richards, respected and valued the South as an area to create vibrant and rich art.

Nineteenth Century

After the American Revolution, the region underwent further change as the nineteenth century brought the rise of the cotton industry. Greatly influenced by the painters of Europe, Romanticism appeared in the Southern art scene just before the Civil War. Artists such as T. Addison Richards, Charles Fraser, John Gaddy Chapman, and David Johnson painted in styles influenced by the passion, nature, human nature, and folklore that encompass the style of Romanticism. Similar to the Hudson River School, the style depicted the innocence and beauty of the South in landscape and in its people.

Throughout the Pre-Civil War period, abolitionists commissioned the work of African American artists and sponsored trips for them to study abroad in Europe. African American art during this time was not limited to the free black community as "slaves were responsible for much of the artistic production of the antebellum period. Even though their anonymity has made it difficult to identify the work of specific black craftsmen, their importance as part of the artisan trades, especially in the South, is unquestionable" (Patton, S.F., 1998, p. 56). At the same time the tensions between the North and South became fierce, and artists found it difficult to find work as economic growth had slowed considerably in most cities.

Painting and sketching outdoors, a popular pastime, became almost impossible once the Civil War started in 1861. Conrad Wise Chapman is an exception to this, as he created paintings of the forts and batteries around Charleston harbor while enlisted in the Confederate Army. When the war ended in 1865, the prosperous southern infrastructure and economy had been significantly damaged, and the landscape of the culture had changed. Photography was used to document and share images of the war, and photojournalism began to emerge out of this new art form. Photographer George S. Cook, who moved to the confederate city of Charleston just before the war, was responsible for the circulation of photographic images throughout the region. His work captured the devastation of Charleston and Fort Sumter throughout the war.

The end of slavery created opportunities for African Americans in the arts. "Whenever possible, African Americans followed the same career path as whites. They had professional art training, the European Grand Tour, patrons, critical acceptance, and public visibility by means of local or regional art exhibitions and viewing" (Patton, S.F, p. 58).

During Reconstruction, landscapes and genre paintings were popular. Genre paintings focused on rural life of the South and the classic characters we think of, such as the southern belle. The expansion of railroads, mechanization of industry, and the rise of coal and steel industries served as inspiration for artists, as well as a national marketplace to compare and contrast works.

Twentieth Century

The twentieth century signaled a shift from rural to urban, and landscape was rejected for the figurative. American modernism swept the country at the turn-of-the-century, with cities like Atlanta, Georgia, and Birmingham, Alabama, became major centers of industry.

While Southern artists continued to celebrate their regional roots and stories through their work, they were continually conscious and affected by the changing visual dialogue of Europe. In particular, southern artists found German expressionism quite inspiring. Lamar Dodd created works during this time that reflected the transitions from naturalism, expressionism, to abstract art, through the eyes of a southern artist. Dodd pulls his imagery from past periods of art and incorporates them into new genres.

Over the years, southern artists have taken German expressionism, transformed it, and made it into their own art form, reflective of their cultural experiences during the South in the 1900s. Continually evolving, this unique form of expressionism is experiencing a revival, as the New American Southern Expressionist movement, which is a contemporary movement in the South today.

In contrast to mainstream modernism and social realism, American scene painting, also known as regionalism, became a popular style from the 1920s-1950. Rejecting the modern trends shown by the Armory Show, it focused primarily on depicting a simpler way of life in the small towns and cities of America, instead of making political and social statements.

A leading figure in Charleston's Renaissance in the arts from 1915-1940 was Alice Ravenel Huger Smith. In 1936, Smith painted *Ready for Harvest*, depicting a solitary black woman in a pose gazing at a field. This work was one of thirty watercolors created for a book called *A Carolina Rice Plantation*. Smith's work was inspired by her family's remembrances, especially her grandmother's, and their lives in the South. Smith did not study in Europe or New York as some artists had. She stayed in the South to create her watercolors. As a result, she was able to truly capture the changes and shifts in mood of Carolina over time

Two decades after Charleston's Renaissance, Miami also experienced an important shift in culture and art. Beginning in 1959, the Cuban community in Miami grew by the thousands, and Cuban exiles created a thriving artists community, with Coral Gables as the focal point for Cuban-American art. La Vieja Guardia (the old guard) was the first group of working Cuban artists in Miami, known for creating work with a sense of nostalgia that carried on the artistic traditions they had known in Cuba. Artists such as Baruj Salinas and Rafael Soriano were heavily influenced by their Cuban identity, experiences of exile, and their contact with the mainstream art of the time. Many generations of Cuban artists would follow after LaVieja Guardia. Contemporary artists, such as Maria Brito and Demi, have continued to be influenced by their own cultural history, personal identity, and experiences of exile. Miami has become a thriving international center for art, largely because of these Cuban and Latin American artists who shaped the region.

Towards the end of the century, a rise in post-modernism changed the way we define and understand art. It emphasized the importance of art being inclusive rather than exclusive and focused on the way we produce, view, and comprehend art. Concentrating on its connection to cultural and social changes, this movement allowed for all individuals to interpret art and its cultural context: not just historians or curators. This post-modernist shift was not only important in the southern art world, but it also signified a change in the global society as we entered the new millennium.

Where We Are Now

The southern United States has become one of the most thriving regions for art in the country. The states of Alabama,

Florida, Georgia, North Carolina, South Carolina, Virginia, and West Virginia are home to hundreds of major museums and galleries dedicated to the preservation of art, culture, and education. One of the most important art shows in the United States, Art Basel, is held each year in Miami, Florida, indicating the significance of the southern United States in the national and global art community.

Because of the key role the region has played in the history of the United States and the world, southern art is a distinct and diverse genre that is difficult to label or describe. Art has the unique ability to transcend all boundaries, provoke thought, and create dialogue. The landscape of the South is extraordinary and forever changing, allowing the art of this region to remain unique, to flourish, and continue intriguing the rest of world.

Paula Allen is a painter, sculptor, and illustrator living in St. Petersburg, Florida. She is also the creator and lead artist of Pollyzoom and focuses on large public art collaborations with communities and organizations. Her art has shown nationally and internationally in both public and private collections.

Bibliographical References

Bosch, Lynette M. F. *Cuban-American Art in Miami: Exile, Identity, and the Neo Baroque*. Hampshire, United Kingdom and Burlington, Vermont: Lund Humphries, 2004.

Charleston Renaissance Gallery, The. "Fine Art of the American South." Alice Ravenel Huger Smith, © 2008 Hickins Galleries LLC (http://charlestonrenaissancegallery.com).

Cook, George S. "Through the Lens of Time," Virginia Commonwealth University. Accessed through VCU's Library Digital Collections (http://dig.library.vcu.edu/cdm4/index_cook.php?CISOROOT=/cook)

Morris Museum of Art (www.themorris.org).

Patton, Sharon F. *Oxford History of Art: African-American Art*. London, United Kingdom: Oxford University Press, 1998. pp. 56-58.

Poesch, Jessie. *The Art of the Old South, Painting, Sculpture, Architecture & the Products of Craftsmen 1560-1860*. New York, New York: Alfred A. Knopf, 1983.

Introduction

Unlike the Yankees with their industrial and business fervor and belief in the value of education, Pre-Civil War Southern whites and their descendants, by contrast, lived preponderantly rural lives, whether they lived in the Piedmont or the Tidewater. Their lives were organized around crop cycles, life in small towns, and churches. Marketable crops such as tobacco, rice, and cotton kept them tied to the land.

The southern economy generated great wealth; southern cotton exports helped finance early nineteenth century economic growth. Unfortunately, the South relied so heavily on its agriculture-based economy that it failed to develop urban centers for commerce, finance, industry, and transportation. Even after World War I, when the blacks who supported the war hoped to gain economic and social status and most whites hoped to maintain the racial status quo, the Industrial Revolution challenged the traditional way of life in the South. Most Southerners made their living through growing and maintaining crops; they met at churches and at the courthouse square; they hunted, partied, and worked. Although Southerners recognized that business and industry provided opportunities, it took several generations before the South was able to improve its industry and transportation base.

During the 1920s, southern fortunes further declined. Once the Depression struck, many went broke and became sharecroppers or fled north or west in search of opportunity. In 1941, James Agee and Walker Evans, a writer and photographer, published *Let Us Now Praise Famous Men*, which records the lives of three white sharecropping families sunk in poverty. Evans' portfolio of these gaunt-faced families and their derelict shanties mourns the passing of the southern culture.

It was World War II that led to the emergence of the South from a rural society. As it moved slowly into a new way of life, it had to deal with the end of the sharecropping system, the turbulence of equal rights, and school integration. Although the South has moved away from its conflicted history and shed some of its customs, its artists, musicians, and writers often look to its rich traditions of story telling to recapture its more romantic past.

My intent in undertaking *100 Artists of the South* was to take a fresh look at the magical and insightful ways in which the area's artists have interpreted life in this region with its moonlight and magnolia landscape. How does their art portray living among the moss-draped live oaks, antebellum houses, and the kudzu? How do they look at the South with its slow easy way of life that reaches out, entices you, and holds you mesmerized. Who knows which one of today's emerging artists will have that seminal and ongoing role in preserving, promoting, and interpreting the South's art and culture as a critical part of America's legacy and vision? Is there a Romare Beardon, Jasper Johns, Mose Tolliver, Alice Ravenel Huger Smith, or Lamar Dodd among them?

For me, these artists not only tell the stories of today but also create the excitement for tomorrow. Like today's authors, they are delineating our stories for future generations. In this newest book, I tried to include a variety of art; after all, not everyone works in oil; not everyone paints pictures of Florida water scenes or hand turns wood? I talked to gallery owners and museum workers; I trolled the Internet state-by-state, society-by-society; I read bios, awards, lists of shows; I looked at many different artists. I wanted those who would bring strength, excitement, passion, and variety to this book. I wanted to bring attention to the talent of Alabama, Florida, Georgia, North and South Carolina, and Virginia and West Virginia and show how these different regions inform their work. From coastal plains to the Appalachian Mountains and the piney woods, the South encompasses a wide variety of regions that differ geographically, economically, and politically. These twenty-first century artists portray this southern world in pastels, clay, wood, and other contemporary mediums.

The South is rich with artists. I could have easily produced a book with two hundred artists and still not have exhausted the talent to be found in the region. Art appreciation is highly individual, and some of your favorite artists may not appear in this book. I hope to introduce you to some new and exciting artists; some may already be famous and some may be just emerging.

Art moves on — just like we do. Hopefully, you will enjoy your perusal of this book and learn about and enjoy the South as seen by these artists!

Dan Bynum

On many occasions, during my childhood, I would lay on a hardwood floor while flipping through the latest Sears catalog. The black and white illustrations were a catalyst that awakened my imagination. My current body of work is a distillery of idiosyncrasies and archetypes from my childhood in a Birmingham, Alabama, neighborhood. In my recall mode, visual elements are morphed into a scene from a silent movie, resulting in a tale of human interaction. In many of my works, vintage wallpaper is used to suggest the interior soul of a home and ourselves. I work on a surface over and over, leaving faint traces of the past. I am erasing and reworking, building up layers of images, much like my childhood friends and I did on the sidewalk. Somewhere between the hardwood floor, the neighborhood sidewalk, and today, my artwork can be found.

With his *Backyard Conqueror*, an acrylic, charcoal, and collage on wood panel.

Sidewalk Sociability. Acrylic, charcoal, collage on wood panel, 24" x 24", 2010.

Sweet Mother Earth. Acrylic and charcoal on wood panel, 24" x 24", 2010.

House of Open Minds. Charcoal and collage on wood
panel, 10" x 47" ea., 2009.

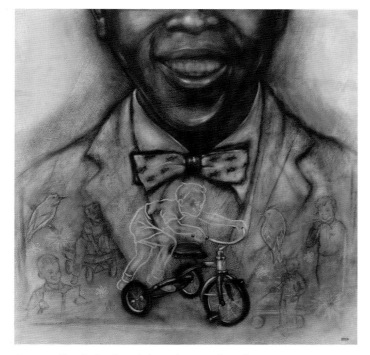

Imaginary Friends. Acrylic and charcoal on wood panel,
24" x 24", 2010.

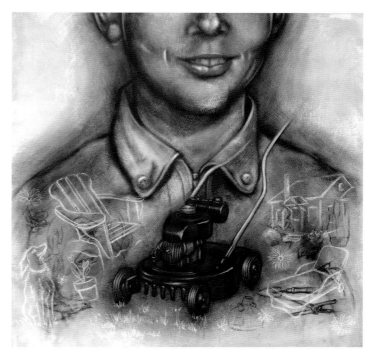

Surveying the World of Work. Acrylic and charcoal on wood panel, 24"
x 24", 2010.

Gary Chapman

I am an artist. I draw, paint, print, sculpt, find, and assemble my work. I am a realist; however, I am not interested in the simple reproduction of an image. I am interested in a realism that goes beyond pictorial reality and recognizes a broader and deeper understanding of what real means. In this realism, feelings, ideas, and emotions are as tangible as an apple or a face. Although I make images, I am not a camera.

In my work, I attempt to dig deeper in the investigation as to what is real and what is truth. As an artist, I do not limit myself or my subjects to a single moment in time or place. Nor do I limit my interpretation of them through just one medium, device, or style. It is through this expanded visual vocabulary and the cathartic process that I hope to reveal a more complete and genuine understanding of my subjects.

Of all my professional accomplishments, I am most proud of the museum acquisitions. As of 2011, a total of twelve paintings have been purchased for the permanent collections of ten museums in the southeast region.

Re-Engage. Oil on canvas, inserted into wooden panels with mixed media, 84" x 64", 2010.

Re Creation. Oil and gold leaf on canvas, inserted into wooden panels with mixed media, 84" x 64", 2008.

Fly Boy. Oil and gold leaf on canvas, inserted into wooden panels with mixed media, 31" x 43", 2009.

X + Y = Z. Oil and gold leaf on canvas, inserted into wooden panels with mixed media, 31" x 43", 2007.

To Be With You. Oil and gold leaf on canvas, inserted into wooden panels with mixed media, 84" x 64", 2011.

Drew Galloway

Growing up in the South, I spent a good bit of my childhood playing in and exploring nearby creeks and lakes. This early fascination with water and its endless aesthetic variations has led me to use the creeks and streams familiar to anyone in the region as my primary subject matter. Painting on collaged metal allows me to create collaboration between my intentions as an artist and the inherent beauty of the material.

Creek Study. Oil on collaged metal, 46" x 60", 2008.

Cathedral. Oil on collaged metal, 48" x 48", 2010.

Still Life #4. Oil on collaged metal, 52" x 44", 2008.

Water Study (Stained Glass). Oil on metal, 46" x 70", 2008.

Dale Kennington

Like Picasso, I really think that painting is another way of keeping a diary. If I kept a diary, I think that it would be rather unremarkable, for my life has not been characterized by a series of crises. It has consisted of many routine days and nights spent with friends and family, dealing with the usual problems and pleasures. Perhaps because of this, I am convinced that our lives are ultimately shaped not by the few cataclysmic events that happen to each of us, but by the everyday things we do — those moments that we couldn't place individually because each one fades into the next. It's only when we look back on years of such moments that they merge into a comprehensive memory that allows us to draw conclusions about our society and ourselves. Each of these comprehensive or "whole" memories is what I think of as a "common ritual"; something that recurs on an ongoing basis, be it once a month, once a week, or once a year. While we pursue some rituals alone, those that seem to shape our destiny and define us as people are collective. The individual has significance not so much because of his individuality but rather because he is a part of the great human community.

Having spent my entire life in the South, I am very aware of rituals, easily recognized or not. The language that we Southerners use is filled with nuances that take years to truly learn. We find our destiny through ties — not coercive ties placed upon us, but by ties we freely choose. These ties are the subject of my work. What I see when I paint is unique to me; what the viewer sees in the same painting is also unique. We are each influenced by the intimate personal mythologies we bring to the work.

The Birthday Party. Oil on canvas, 42" x 84", 2003.

Exit. Oil on canvas, 48" x 40", 2003.

A Question of Survival. Six-panel folding screen, oil on wood panel, 94" x 144", recto, 2005-2007.

The Debutantes. Oil on canvas, 52" x 72", 2000.

John Douglas Powers

The allure of the unattainable and its connection to the passage of time have become central to my research. Drawing from areas as diverse as natural history, architecture, and the history of technology, I am engaged in an investigation of what lies at the intersection of cinema, computation, music, and physical space. I often employ motion and sound in my work, incorporating the passage of time as a compositional element in an attempt to more closely examine abstract and often intangible topics such as memory, thought, emotion, language, and the essence of self.

Faust. Wood, steel, paper, electric motors, typewriter, and 2-channel pinhole animation, dimensions variable, 2010.

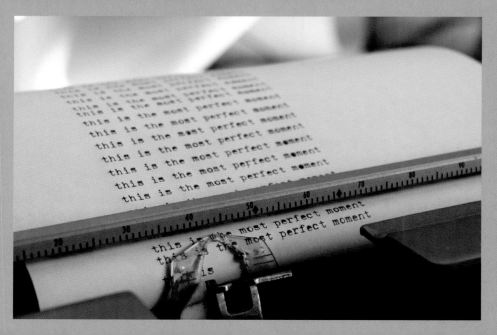

Field of Reeds. Wood, steel, plastic, and electric motor;
4-1/2' x 14' x 12', 2008.

Lethe. Wood, steel, aluminum, two-way mirror, and
electric motor, 8" x 8" x 8", 2009.

Omphalos. Marble and feathers, 90" x 24" x 8", 2010.

Jerry Siegel

I am a strong believer in place, and how a region, community, and a home will shape who you become. The place I know, where I was raised, is Selma, Alabama, in the Black Belt region of the American South. It is how I was raised, instilled with belief in family and tradition that motivates me to document the place I call home. I am passionate about exploring and examining this region and its people. I travel to small towns, rural areas, and back roads to capture the essence of my southern roots. My intent is to use photography as a narrative to depict the South I have always known as well as the new look of the South as it moves forward through changes because of poverty, the exodus from rural areas, and the ambiguous economics of the area. I strive to depict this area with the reality as I see it and the emotions that accompany it.

Revival tent, Creola, Alabama. Archival inkjet print, 40" x 26", 2009.
Courtesy of Barbara Archer Gallery.

Deer heads, Perry County, Alabama. Archival inkjet print, 40" x 26", 2002. *Courtesy of Barbara Archer Gallery.*

Painted bus with Dog, Selma, Alabama. Archival inkjet print, 40" x 26", 2005. *Courtesy of Barbara Archer Gallery.*

Ticket booth, Central Alabama Fair, Dallas County, Alabama. Archival inkjet print, 40" x 26", 2007. *Courtesy of Barbara Archer Gallery.*

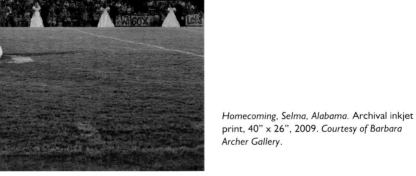

Homecoming, Selma, Alabama. Archival inkjet print, 40" x 26", 2009. *Courtesy of Barbara Archer Gallery.*

2.
Florida

Paula Allen

Art is a language many of us have spoken since we were children. As artists, we continue to speak that language, and, like all linguists, the more we speak it the more familiar we are and the further we advance in our skills. Sharing our talents with people through imagery is an honorable and important part of the legacy of art and the life of an artist. My images included on these pages were created in October 2009, a few months before the oil spill in the Gulf of Mexico. The images included are water spirit characters, who are telling the story of what was about to happen to their world and our world. I created the images with watercolors and India ink, over a three-week period and put them away. When the oil spill occurred months later, I understood the story of the water spirits. The watercolors were expressing the world of the creatures in the water and how their world was going to be destroyed.

Art can be a way of communicating intuitive ideas, a way to bring attention to a problem through a story, or by creating something beautiful out of something tragic. Art has healing abilities through its color and imagery that can help people come back into balance. The artists can be healed through the creation; viewing the art can heal the viewer. Aboriginal cultures have always used this; we have forgotten and have to remember. We have collectively forgotten the uses of art, but many of us are remembering. Creativity is not just for artists; it's a gift from the universe to everyone.

Courtesy of Carol Gallagher.

Mama Pacha. Watercolor, mixed media, 24" x 31", 2009.

Water Spirit Family. Watercolor, mixed media, 24" x 31", 2009.

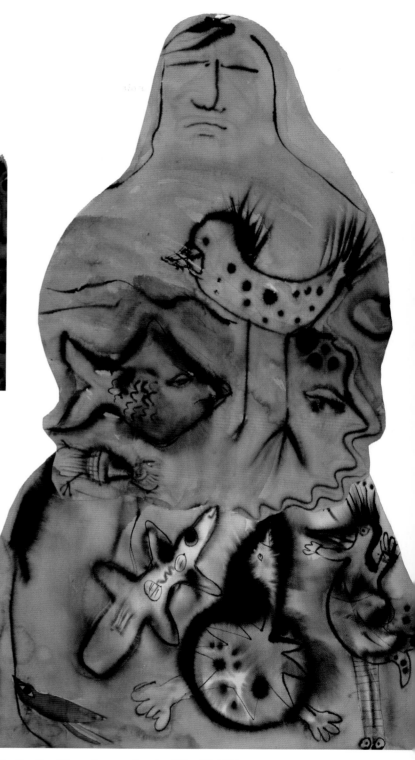

The Guardian. Watercolor, mixed media, 25" x 41", 2009.

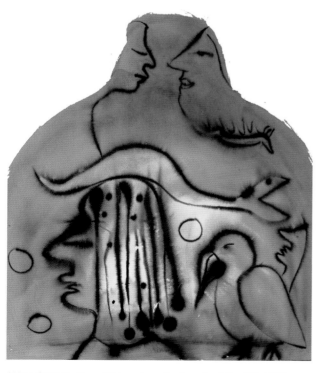

Water Spirit Marriage. Watercolor, mixed media, 24" x 31", 2009.

Gwenneth Barth-White

I'll be drawn instinctively towards a certain person in a certain light situation; the mystery of human existence is at the root of my fascination: its ephemeral and paradoxically eternal quality. Art targets the multiple and translucent layers of perception and what we see.

I love painting, I think about it all the time. In the daytime, it's a riddle, an intriguing mystery that needs to be solved. How? At night, I'll dream that I've discovered some wonderful fabulous thing — like a treasure of diamonds — that will change all known perceptions about painting. My dreams are multi-colored, multi-dimensional, fabulously detailed, and visually gorgeous — if only I could paint them! Someday, someday I'll capture that. Artists are addicts, addicted to finding something that only their solitary intuition tells them exists.

Florida, with its beautiful light, its raw intensity, and the feeling that the jungle, the wild life, is a heartbeat underneath, dispels the staid grayness of the Geneva that I grew up in. That's a start.

After Supper. Pastel, 32" x 20", 2010. *Courtesy of André Longchamp Geneva.*

Tea and Geraniums. Pastel, 20" x 20", 2009. Courtesy of André Longchamp Geneva.

St. Florent Boats. Pastel, 18" x 13", 2010. *Courtesy of André Longchamp Geneva.*

Je t'attendais. Pastel, 18" x 13", 2010. *Courtesy of André Longchamp Geneva.*

The Orange Cutter. Pastel, 24" x 15-1/4", 2009. *Courtesy of André Longchamp Geneva.*

John Beard

As a boy growing up in Islandmorada, Florida, I spent most of my time exploring the abundance of nature, collecting treasures along the shore, exploring islands, diving, sailing, and fishing. I will forever cherish my childhood in the Keys. I have traveled the world, but my inspiration is rooted in the South.

From the smell of the air, the taste of the salt, and the sound of the waves hitting the shore, painting breathes life into the memories flowing through my mind, expressing something words cannot.

Koi. Acrylic on canvas, 24" x 36", 2011.

Lily Pond. Acrylic on canvas, 48" x 48", 2010.

Portuguese Traffic Jam. Oil on canvas, 48" x 36", 2010.

Bell Tower. Oil on canvas, 48" x 30", 2010.

Positano. Oil on canvas, 16" x 20", 2009.

Peter A. Cerreta

Living in the South, getting away from the maniacal "speed-dial" ways of life in most other regions of the US, has afforded me the luxury to revisit my senses while watching "life in the moment."

I'm a "people watcher." I am drawn not only to how people look, but I also try to sense what people are "inside," what emotions motivate each to action. Then I devise a scenario, leading me to create a "story telling moment in time."

As with most artists, I cannot remain confined to a comfortable way of recording what I see and feel. In an attempt to stay vital and relevant as an artist, I am compelled to find alternative approaches and media to put into a visible form my every changing personal vision. This is the right path for me.

American Gothic Revisited. Acrylic on canvas, 24" x 24".

I'm Simply an Ordinary Lady. Acrylic on canvas, 30" x 40", 2010.

You Can Run But You Can't Hide. Acrylic on canvas, 30" x 40", 2011.

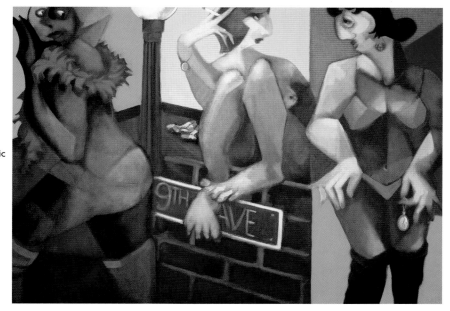

OK, Ladies Let's Go, Time is Money. Acrylic on canvas, 30" x 40", 2011.

There's Always Someone to Wage War. Acrylic on canvas, 30" x 40", 2011.

Dolores Coe

To grow up on the narrow peninsula of Florida is to be steeped in a cultural mix and match, human and animal migration patterns, and whatever else is left behind. It has long been the land of racing toward, or away, from something — the lost and found. One side short of being an island, it is both paradise and a harsh, sometimes violent environment. It is a rich Petri dish that I have long observed, documented, and responded to.

In paint and in mixed media, I construct invented spaces inhabited by iconic and culturally familiar elements that are spun into new contexts and discovered narratives. Photographing common cultural icons, iconic events, and places fuels the imagery: yard statuary, architectural kitsch, parking lot carnivals, and religious iconography. I am intrigued by their endless replication, their constant variation, the contexts in which I find them and their cross-cultural migration.

I travel widely collecting sources and inspiration for my work that is informed by my interest in poetry, documentary forms, and new media processes. These sources become a palette of fragments. I discover in them an abrupt juxtaposition of quite different elements that generates a starting point. The painting begins here in an open process in which the actual world, space, and other elements are imagined and evolved. Small works reverse the process. These spaces and images are preconceived, like constructing a stage set. I think of them as small narrative moments, built with specificity, but akin to the musings of mind and memory.

The unpopulated, inactive carnival, the stage-set quality of rides and amusement attractions — both retro and futuristic — harkens to an imagined future of another time. It is the experience of this quality, the sense of memory, fantasy, illusion, and the perception of internal experience that I hope to make tangible.

Courtesy of Bruce Marsh.

Carnival Tempest. Oil and oil enamel on linen, 60" x 48", 2008.

Carnival: Sail Away. Oil and oil enamel on linen, 60" x 48", 2008.

Excavating the Sky. Oil on canvas, 66" x 72", 2010.

Surfing with Dante. Oil on canvas, 66" x 72", 2010.

Fun Slide. Oil/ink/gesso on wood panel, 9" x 8", 2008.

Sid Daniels

As a teenager, growing up in suburban Toronto, Canada, during the '60s, I developed a fascination for MGM Hollywood movie musicals and music from the 1930s and '40s. The movies that had a profound impact on my creative imagination were the black and white films that were choreographed by Busby Berkeley during the '30s, together with the technicolor musicals from the 1940s that starred Carmen Miranda (the Brazilian Bombshell) and movie star Betty Grable, who both appeared in *Down Argentine Way*, *Moon Over Miami*, and *The Gang's All Here*. The juxtaposition of euphoric Big Band era swing music and the intoxicating rhythmic beat of Conga-line Brazilian and Cuban music were the catalysts that later spawned my larger-than-life showgirl series of women wearing flamboyant costumes and high heels.

In front of the canvas, I aim for extravagant, provocative images, which move to the music that inspires me. As an artist, I see myself as a contemporary "Toulouse Lautrec." I have appropriately coined my style "Latin Deco," resulting in works of art that I present with a sense of humor and pizzazz. I continue my passion to create works of art that are directly influenced by the world of nostalgia, burlesque, theater, fashion, and dance. I have learned that living in a tropical paradise is not to be taken for granted, and in a lot of ways, it's a lot like being on the set of an MGM technicolor movie musical.

Salsa Rainbow. Acrylic, 48" x 48", 2011.

Scheherazade. Acrylic, 48" x 72", 2008.

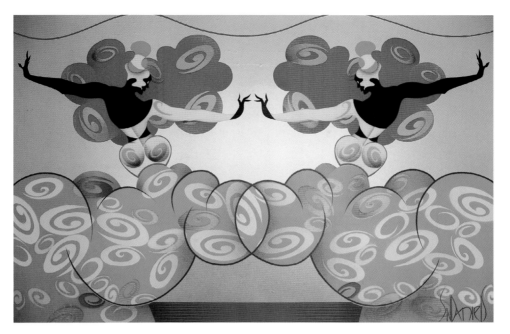

Follies Twins. Acrylic, 84" x 55", 2008.

Fandango Tango. Acrylic, 48" x 60", 2007.

Kalamazoo No.1. Acrylic, 48" x 60", 2007.

Christian Duran

In the pursuit of inspiration and personal growth as a painter, I chose south Florida as my home in 1999. I returned to the South from Kansas City to discover an exciting energy and emergence within the art community. In addition, I believe that the tropical atmosphere and Hispanic culture here have become a focal point in my work. From this, I frequently depict and find insight parallel to my own ambitions.

Mother. Oil on canvas, 35" x 26.5", 2006. *Courtesy of Juan Cabrera.*

Apparition. Oil on canvas, 65" x 54", 2006. *Courtesy of Juan Cabrera.*

Crucifixion After Botticelli Number Two. 30" x 22", 2007.

Maker. Oil on canvas, 35" x 26.5", 2008. *Courtesy of Juan Cabrera.*

Easter. 36" x 36", 2007. *Courtesy of Juan Cabrera.*

Bill Farnsworth

As an illustrator for more than thirty years, I have come to a point in my career where I have one foot still in illustration and the other in fine art. So I feel the narrative part of me is still there and crossing over to the gallery work. Everyday life has a story no matter how small; it deserves telling if it has the right light. The light is what makes something very special or just forgettable. Cool overcast light can have a beautiful soft edge look, while sunny warm light can create interesting patterns and color. In order to get this on canvas and convey it honestly to the viewer, an artist must have the skills of visual language. Having the technical skill will give the artist the ability to express.

If you travel to another country and don't know the language, no one will understand you. This goes for art as well. A painting with bad values, shapes, and edges will not convey to the viewer how the artist feels about the subject. My illustration work over the years has been the best training to put a picture together. Tight deadlines and being asked to paint everything under the sun was a great motivator to be resourceful. So today the learning process continues and with it comes little steps of improvement. For me this is what makes painting so rewarding and fun. Moments in life pass by us all the time; if we can capture the great ones honestly in paint and canvas, then maybe it will make our lives better.

Living in southwest Florida has been a great environment for my art. The beautiful surrounding and easy lifestyle have helped me create some of the best art of my life.

Racing Against the Storm. Oil on canvas, 16" x 18", 2007.

After the Rain. Oil on linen, 18" x 24", 2011.

Cortez Lowtide. Oil on linen. 20" x 24", 2011.

Montauck Point. Oil on linen, 18" x 24", 2011.

Watching The Sun Rise. Oil on linen, 12" x 10", 2011.

Lilian Garcia-Roig

By definition, plein air painting means working on-site, experiencing nature first-hand. My paintings are made directly from life and are documents of a real-time process: the accumulation of fleeting moments, the experience of the day. In the South, the days are long and often hot and moist. My newest large-scale paintings of dense, ordinary landscapes reflect these qualities by overwhelming the viewer's perceptual senses. Each painting is created over the course of the entire day in an intense wet-on-wet cumulative manner. My works are as much about the materiality of the paint and the physicality of the painting process as they are about mixing and mashing the illusionist possibilities of painting with its true abstract nature.

Born in Havana, Cuba, I have spent the last ten years living and working in Tallahassee, Florida, as a professor in the Department of Art at Florida State University and am still amazed and inspired by the extensive lush surroundings in the Big Bend region. I have been included in numerous shows around the country. Among my major awards are a Joan Mitchell Foundation Award in Painting, a Mid-America Arts Alliance/NEA Fellowship Award in Painting, State of Florida Individual Artist Fellowship Award, Kimbrough Award from the Dallas Museum of Art, and fellowship residencies to Skowhegan School of Painting and Sculpture, Vermont Studio Center and MacDowell Colony.

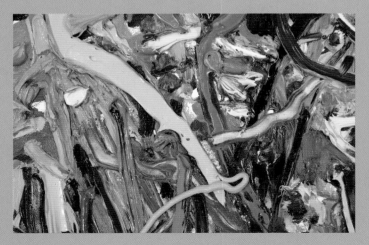

St. Mark's Inlet (FL). Oil on canvas, 40" x 30", 2007.

Hyperbolic Nature: Vine Diptych (FL). Oil on canvas, 60" x 96", 2008.

Palms & Fronds. Oil on canvas, 60" x 48", 2008.

Cumulative Nature: Palm Canopy (FL). Oil on canvas, 48" x 36", 2007.

Dean Gioia

North Florida is my world, where my life unfolds. The beauty here is subtle and graceful. Our geography does not dazzle with mountain vistas or rocky coasts. Rather, it entices and coaxes with canopy roads, hidden creeks, lime-walled rivers, and salt marshes running to the gulf. These things are alternately dressed with stormy summer afternoons, brilliant blue autumns, winter frost, and dogwood springs. The combination of land, weather, and light coalesces into an essence that reaches out, wraps around, and holds you close.

Since early childhood, my attention has been on the motion of life, of day becoming night, spring becoming summer, the phases of the moon, and the constantly changing miracle of illumination. Sometime around the age of twelve, painting became my way of expressing my feelings about the world. I have always had a sense of a grand scheme, an earthly machine slowly and methodically working, spinning, revolving, moving through darkness and light. I am a passenger on this ride watching the spectacle of light unfold each day across my north Florida home with extraordinary complexity and beauty. My art has always been a prayer of thanks and praise for the splendid journey.

Courtesy of Richard's Photography, Tallahassee, Florida.

Morning in the Field. Acrylic on canvas, 24" x 36", 2008. Courtesy of Richard's Photography, Tallahassee, Florida.

Middle of Summer. Acrylic on canvas, 24" x 36", 2010. Courtesy of Richard's Photography, Tallahassee, Florida.

Poseys Sunset, 1985. Acrylic on canvas. 24" x 36," 2009. *Courtesy of Richard's Photography, Tallahassee, Florida.*

November Sunrise, St. Marks. Acrylic on canvas, 24" x 36", 2008.
Courtesy of Richard's Photography, Tallahassee, Florida.

Torreya in Summer. Acrylic on canvas, 30" x 40", 2008.
Courtesy of Richard's Photography, Tallahassee, Florida.

Jack Hughes

In art, as in life, if I am unconcerned about where I am, then I am never lost. It's a Southern thing. When I don't edit, I find my best work. I like to think that my paintings are probably what cartoon characters dream about. Art can, and should, be fun — serious fun. If it's serious and fun, who can possibly have a problem with that?

Instinctively, our subconscious assigns order to randomness. I expanded this idea using cultural icons, childhood images, and life observations — counting on the human drive to find meaning. Curiously, some of my fellow artists attribute an almost mystical element to them. The most amazing thing, for me, has been listening to the many differing stories.

I've enjoyed a long and exciting career, from exhibiting at many shows, to being invited to the White House by President and Mrs. Reagan, in 1988. In 1989, I was invited to participate in the White House Easter Egg Exhibit in December. In 2008/January 2009, the Kemper Museum of Contemporary Art hosted a one-man show for my paintings. I am humbled and grateful.

Artist with son Mason Jack Hughes. Painting, *Unameit*, is acrylic on board, 29.75" x 29.75". *Courtesy of Giovanni Lunardi Photography.*

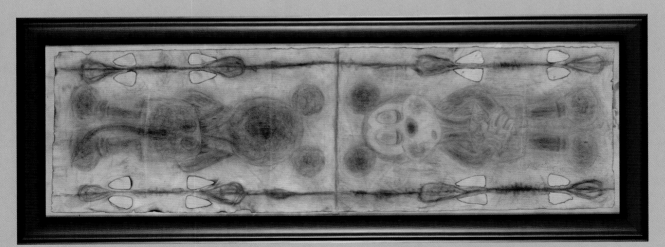

The Shroud of Orlando. Pastel, charcoal, and tea on cotton, 19.25" x 52.5". *Courtesy Giovanni Lunardi Photography.*

Poor Bobo Was Completely Unprepared for the Holy Metallic Invasion. Acrylic on board, 32.5" x 44". *Courtesy of Giovanni Lunardi Photography.*

Without a Net. Acrylic on board, 32" x 44". *Courtesy of Dan Wayne.*

And If…#3. Acrylic on board, 36" x 31". *Courtesy of Giovanni Lunardi Photography.*

Clive King

I work almost exclusively in the area of drawing, mainly graphite on paper, and broadly explore several main themes: autobiographical events, the uneasy relationship between landscape and industry, cultural erosion, and synthesis and the evocation of a sense of place. For the purposes of narrative, many take on a triptych format. At present, they are a constant 80 inches high and 240 inches long.

In 1992 (two days after Hurricane Andrew), I came to Miami from Oxford, England. The images of destruction and the rapid and powerful renewal of both land and people had an immediate and profound effect on my artwork; this, combined with many excursions into the North Carolina mountains, has sponsored the most fertile period of my career.

Most of my work is developed as a series. Some are conceived as a local observation and develop into a much bigger concept, so a triptych on the effects of 9/11 on my immediate environment ("Dispatches from the Nether Regions") becomes a much larger exploration on the Mideast conflict through pieces like "Towers of Babel" and "State of Grace." A new series I have started working on, "The Other Four Corners," explores incidents and issues at four extremities of North America: Newfoundland, Alaska, San Diego, and Miami. In addition to exploring cultural traits and social/ecological problems, they are also a personal document of visiting these vivid locations. One of the pieces has been completed so far, "Dreamers Lust." Like the rest of this series, it is executed in a complex layering of colored inks.

My interest lies more in illusion than physicality, which is why my large pieces are always presented frameless and without glass. I would like them to float like wafers on the wall — without weight they can push you back or pull you in.

Dreamers Lust. Ink on paper, 80" x 80", 2010.

Dreamers Lust. Ink on paper, 80" x 240", 2010.

Towers of Babel. Left. Graphite on paper. 80 x 80." 2008.

Towers of Babel. Center. Graphite on paper, 80" x 80", 2008.

State of Grace. Graphite on paper, 80" x 240", 2009.

State of Grace (center). Graphite on paper, 80" x 80", 2009.

Barbara Krupp

Sunshine equals light. Morning has come, the birds are singing, and the gentle breeze is blowing. The mood has been set. Surrounded by paradise, it is time to pick up the brush. I find that I can now lose myself in my feelings as I paint my abstract paintings. I call them "abstract nature" because although they are abstract, the viewer can see natural forms. When they experience the feeling I have put in the painting, then the painting is complete.

Painting in Florida frees the spirit. I find my color palette changes with the light to a brighter palette, and like my surroundings, gentler. I believe when you dance, the world will dance with you. I listen to the ocean, and the rhythm produces a calming effect on my being. My spirit is sent soaring. After my day's work is done, I go for a walk in my garden. I have designed it with spaces sectioned into rooms similar to my artwork. I have blended life, paintings, and gardens into joy.

Out of This World. Acrylic on canvas, 36" x 60", 2011

Blue Skirt Waltz. Acrylic on canvas, 45" x 65", 2009.

This Time Tomorrow. Acrylic on canvas, 60" x 48," 2011.

On Gossamer Wings. Acrylic on canvas, 36" x 48", 2009.

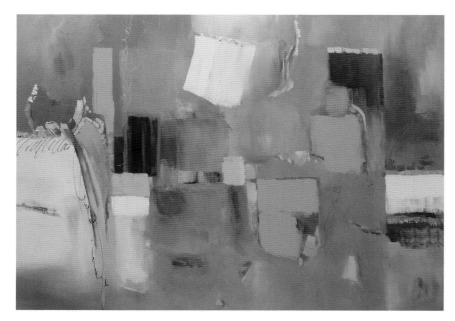

Killarney. Acrylic on canvas, 36" x 48", 2010.

Mernet Larsen

I try to evoke a sense of permanence, solidity, weight, time stopped, and the essences of ordinary events and concrete images filtered through wry detachment. I understand these paintings as makeshift contraptions, statements of recognition that essences and memory must be constructed, invented.

This painted world must be obviously artificial. It reaches toward, not from, life. The characters and objects are geometric solids, their structures and proportions reinvented in tension with the event depicted. I often paint the elements separately on tracing paper, trying out different noses, head, arms, then pasting them on. I want the mechanisms of my paintings to be fully visible: measuring, layering, carving, texturing, coloring, and pasting. I want nonspecific viewpoints, a sense of vertigo, so that you are holding each situation in your mind almost as if you are wearing it. Renaissance, isometric, and reverse perspectives interact.

While I have been immersed in Florida's nature and culture for over fifty years, my work most often depicts my life teaching at the University of South Florida: faculty meetings, seminars, going to the mall. It has also been informed by travel in Japan, China, and Europe, a passionate interest in art history, and a strong connection with New York, where I now spend almost half of every year.

Mall Event. Acrylic/tracing paper on canvas, 50" x 55", 2010.

Seminar. Acrylic/tracing paper on canvas, 59" x 40", 2011.

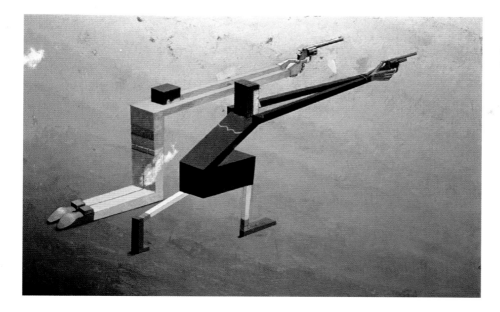

Gunfighters. Acrylic/tracing paper/oil on canvas, 44" x 68", 2001.

Committee. Acrylic/tracing paper on canvas, 36" x 68", 2007.

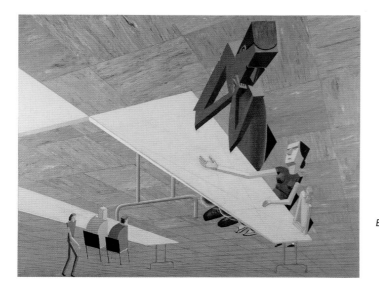

Explanation. Acrylic/tracing paper on canvas, 41" x 52", 2007.

Luisa Mesa

The inspiration for my work arises from a strong desire to connect with a deeper part of myself. Line, repetition, and layering are fundamental in the work — every one of my pieces begins with a layer of repetitive drawing. The lines in the work are a metaphor for the inter-connectedness of all things, and the multiple layers allude to the multidimensionality of our existence.

My choice and combination of colors are spontaneous, at times marrying colors that are not complementary but somehow work together. Cuban by birth, and living and working in the southernmost part of the United States, such as Miami, Florida, undoubtedly influences my palette. I am not shy when choosing color and have a tendency to work in different shades of blues, greens, and reds, to name some. I work in various media such as enamel, spray paint, digital images, and resin.

All the photographs that appear in some of my work have personal meaning, generating "worlds," both imagined and real, by digitally combining different imagery.

The installations I create symbolize our perceived individuality and how at a deeper level everything is connected to everything else. Every piece that makes up each installation is different, yet together they constitute a whole.

With *Evolution*, mixed media on wood panels, 2010.

Transcending. Enamel markers, acrylic, digital image, and resin on wood panel, 24" x 60" x 4", 2010.

48

Meditations on Transcending. Enamel markers and oil on wood panel, 26" x 26" x 2", 2010.

In Flux. Archival ink and enamel markers on clay board, 12" x 12" x 2", 2010.

Midnight. Enamel markers, acrylic, lenses, and resin on wood panel, 30" x 3", 2007.

Empowered. Ultrachrome print on diasec mount, 24" x 29", 2011.

Roger Palmer

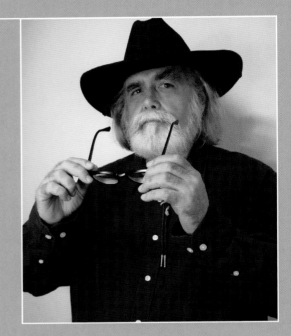

I grew up in the wild and domesticated world of ranch and swamp. I walked in a herd of cattle. Alligators walked past nervous cows.

A drawing is a herd of marks.

My grandfather kept us alive through sheer bad-ass brilliant control and his charm and reputation as a storyteller. Stories were not often told in whole form to small boys, but they could be seen wrapped on the table, penciled on the butcher paper that had blood under it. The adults stopped in mid-sentence to send you out of the room.

Perspective space was a knothole under the floor.

A vanishing point was when they could not see you.

I draw with a Ronin Zenga Southern Dog Without Papers attitude. I want to be on the white page and roll in the flow of some backwater storyline. The mortal page. With accidents of wit, chaos trimmed out of the ordinary day to find a funny bone inside the brush.

Creationism Gets Examined By Dogs. Pure pigments/acrylic on rag paper, 26" x 40", 2007.

She Knew About Death And Scrambled Eggs, But Plucking Before Killing Was Torture, So She Took Her Egg And Ran For It.
Pure pigments/acrylic on rag paper, 36" x 36", 2009.

Fat Cats Worry About Class Warfare. Pure pigments/acrylic on rag paper, 26" x 20", 2011.

Country Cannon. Pure pigments/acrylic on rag paper, 26" x 40", 2006.

Places Where They Hang You For Singing Off Key With Your Dog. Pure pigments/acrylic on rag paper, 50" x 42", 2008.

Slow Battle Field. Pure pigments/acrylic on rag paper, 50" x 40", 2008.

Tere Pastoriza

The South is north of here — everybody knows that. If I want to see dogwoods and magnolias, or sink my teeth into a luscious fried green tomato, I have to either get in my car and drive north or close my eyes and go inward.

I spend a lot of time there: inward that is. It is a glorious place where the imagination resides and a treasure trove of wisdom is stored. It is where I draw, paint, and mix one media with another. It's where I question, ponder, and occasionally find an answer. It is where time and boundaries disappear, where universal laws rule, and where everything points in the same direction.

When I open my eyes, I find myself south of the South, north, east and west of the ocean, right smack in the middle of the city, where amid Royal Poincianas and palm trees I spot a white ibis, in this a very familiar albeit strange land: Miami.

"Untitled," from the *Until I Grow Wings* series.
Graphite on Mylar, 10" x 8", 2011.

Angelica. Graphite drawing on vellum layered over photographic images encased in glass and resin, 3-1/2" diameter, 2006.

Jessica. Graphite drawing on vellum layered over photographic images encased in glass and resin, 3-1/2" diameter, 2006.

Kenya. Graphite drawing on vellum layered over photographic images encased in glass and resin, 3-1/2" diameter, 2006.

Queen of Clubs. Graphite on Mylar, 60" x 42", 2009.

Barbara Rivera

I was born in Puerto Rico and then came with my family to Miami in 1987. Here I studied at the University of Miami, where I received my BFA in painting, and then at Florida International University, where I received my MFA. I am still living in Miami.

I'm inspired by paintings from the eighteenth century, particularly from the Victorian era, mainly because of the significant abundance of that time and the female force behind it. I create images that provide a contemporary version of the tradition of decorative, fancy pictures of this era called "Keepsake" (small engraved illustrations of lovely young women). By reconsidering these iconic female images, I create a playful and confrontational version of the traditional female icon. All of my characters are Hispanic by name and by nature, which is my own culture and one that envelops this city. My latest paintings are now in larger scale, and still focusing on the same concept, now in a more confrontational way.

Artist with works in progress *Rubí* and *Petulas* (series *Que dulce*).

Untitled (gummy worms). Oil on canvas, 9" x 6", 2006.

Untitled (cotton candy). Oil on canvas, 9" x 6", 2006.

Tomasa, Adora y Abigail. Oil on board, 30" x 24", 2010.

Sara y Pilar. Oil on board, 30" x 24", 2009-10.

Xochilt, Virinia. Oil on board, 4" x 4" ea., 2008.

Mark Rutkowski

I came down to South Florida in 1983 to do a series of watercolors of the Art Deco District of Miami Beach, an area that was threatened with demolition. The bright sunlight on stucco surface lent well to the watercolor medium as well as the scale I was working in. I eventually moved to Miami Beach in 1992, partnering in a mural business and continuing to paint the watercolors in a small storefront on Espanola Way. The lively colors of South Florida have continued to influence me. After more than 250 paintings of the Art Deco District, I have added an oil painting studio, where I paint the ocean and clouds of southern Florida,

I began the assemblages while working in my studio in France in 2002. They consist of many individual postcard-sized canvases assembled on a large panel. This series continues in the Miami Beach studio today.

Great Cloud of Unknowing. Oil, acrylic on canvas board panel, 30" x 96", 2006.

Past. Oil on canvas board panel, 48" x 72", 2003.

Carlyle at Night. Watercolor on paper, 49" x 24", 2009.

Cavalier at Dusk. Watercolor on paper, 44" x 33", 1996.

The Crown. Watercolor on paper, 52" x 20", 2011.

Claudia G. Thomas

An endless variety of subject matter exists in Florida, along with year-round mild temperatures and countless days of bright sunlight. In other words, a plein air artist's paradise! While enjoying the outdoors, my goal is to capture the natural effects of light and changing color throughout the day and interpret what inspires me. For that inspiration, I look to lush botanical gardens, various species of palm and fruit trees, exotic flowers, the water reflections of private boathouses, and the nearby Atlantic Ocean. I spend time in parks with natural springs and around lakes linked by scenic canals. I see Spanish moss, particularly challenging to represent on canvas, draped in aged oak and cypress trees, appearing almost transparent as the sunlight changes it from gray to lavender, yellow ochre, and mint green. White egrets, ibis, and gray herons are also in the local landscape; when in flight with their elongated wings, they are so graceful.

I am challenged more by creating a "closed" landscape, which is abstract and depicts detailed nature scenes up close, than an "open" landscape, which is concerned with atmosphere and distance. I look for subject matter that is both in light and shadow for dramatic contrast, and I search for unusual shapes and color combinations. My oil paintings are brightly colored because nature is a full color spectrum in the South, and every shade of green you can imagine must be part of the palette.

Palm Dance. Oil on canvas, 30" x 22", 2010.

Yellow Frond. Oil on canvas, 22" x 28", 2010.

Criss Cross Palm. Oil on canvas, 24" x 24", 2011.

Narrow Canal. Oil on canvas, 24" x 24", 2010.

Botanical Beauty. Oil on canvas, 30" x 36", 2011.

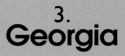
Betsy Cain

I am a daughter of the South, born in Tuscaloosa and raised in Birmingham, Alabama. My parents both came from agrarian backgrounds, and I have indelible impressions of visiting my grandparents' farms as a child. The land of the South is the bedrock of my painting — I am grounded here; however, I have since migrated to Georgia with my husband, David Kaminsky. We live next to the marsh, on the edge of the continent. It is a powerfully visual and profound place to be. The Low Country, as it is called, has infused my painting with its liquidity, density, and humidity. It is a verdant place for metaphor and history — and for the making of art.

My paintings internalize the memory landscape of my past and the perceived landscape that I now inhabit. I like to explore the "zone" between figuration and abstraction, using abstracted elements from the physical landscape combined with the interior landscape of the mind/body. There is often a point where the resolution of an idea/image lingers, hovering before becoming known. This non-literal suggestive state is often where my paintings end up, allowing the viewer a multiplicity of possibilities.

Sino-slide. Oil on board, 60" x 48", 2008.

Tidewater. Oil on board, 48" x 40", 2010.

Nerve flower. Oil on canvas, 60" x 60", 2009.

Isle of elongation #1. Oil on canvas, 60" x 60", 2009.

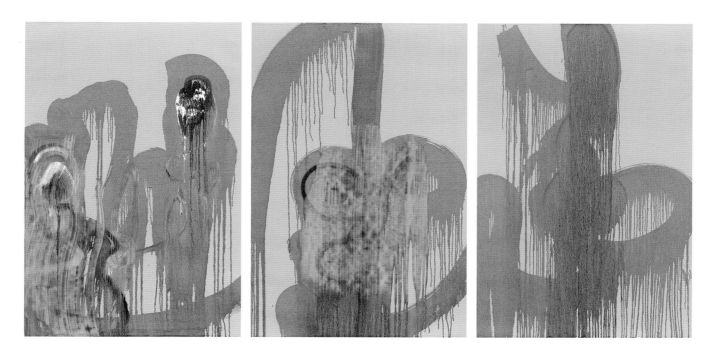

Driptych. Oil on paper, 48" x 96", 2009.

Philip Carpenter

Color pencil drawings replaced painting for me ten years ago, but the processes are similar in that each drawing requires its own painterly invention to describe new surfaces and to create effective illusions. In the drawings, I have moved from singular portraits of ordinary things (e.g. tools, flowers, toys) to images combining my interests in the prosaic and the precious: trash and treasure. I continue to use dolls and action figures acquired by rummaging through thrift store refuse, my ongoing back-door survey of our disposable culture. These figures are alien to me; I don't watch television, and I've never been to Disney World. Previous to using them in my work, I had studiously insulated myself from such, and I find my outsider's detachment an advantage in selecting the objects. I pair these pop culture icons with facsimiles of traditional works of art, with both depicted actual size as often as I can. Employing my knack for mimicry that I've developed copying paintings to demonstrate techniques to my students, I meticulously render the objects and the facsimiles as my way of knowing them fully. Each combination is developed intuitively and individually. They are alike in obvious ways, but they are often centuries apart. Fine art encounters popular culture; the ideal meets mockery — the frequency of religious themes seems particularly southern to me. Other combinations are less pointed, more poetic, and inexplicably (in)appropriate.

Courtesy of Daryl White.

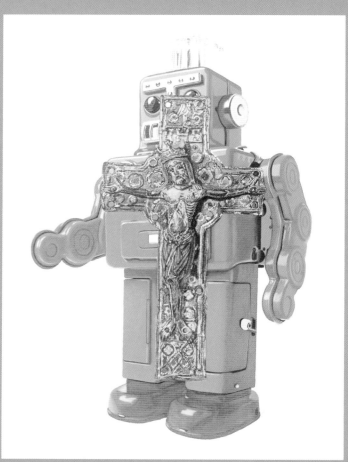

Art in America. Color pencils on paper, 2007. *Courtesy of Marcia Wood Gallery.*

Ecce Homo. Color pencils on paper, 24" x 20", 2009. *Courtesy of Marcia Wood Gallery.*

After Durer. Color pencils on paper, 24" x 20", 2009.
Courtesy of Marcia Wood Gallery.

Innocents. Color pencils on paper, 24" x 20", 2007.
Courtesy of Marcia Wood Gallery.

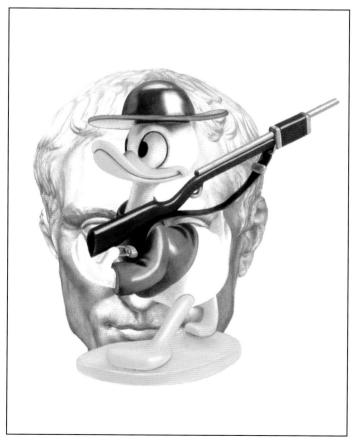

Hero. Color pencils on paper, 24" x 20", 2009.
Courtesy of Marcia Wood Gallery.

Visitation. Color pencils on paper, 2010.
Courtesy of Marcia Wood Gallery.

Mary Engel

The first intentional burials with ritual objects occurred 35,000 years ago and, with them, the first expressions of human faith appeared. A predominant burial image was the animal. The use of ritualized animal images has had enduring religious, mythic, and aesthetic significance. The animal image (especially the dog) is central to my work and philosophy. For me, the animal image symbolizes a bridge between the rational world of humans and the instinctual world of nature.

My dogs, Mingo and Bonnie, come to my studio everyday to "pose" (sleep and play). My sculptural goal is to capture an animal's gesture or movement. The surfaces of the sculptures are rich in texture and refer to human creations, memory, and patterns. African grave markers and old southern memory jars have inspired these exterior embellishments. The titles come from charm bracelets, pins, or other objects with names. Through my work, I aspire to create whimsical animated creatures that reveal a spiritual presence I feel animals possess.

Artist with Mingo, Bonnie, and Louise.
Courtesy of Carlo Nasisse.

Watch Dog. Mixed media, hydrocal, epoxy, watches, 9" x 22" x 7", 2010. *Courtesy of Carlo Nasisse.*

Elliot. Mixed media, ceramic, decals, epoxy, and found objects,
14" x 10" x 7", 2010. *Courtesy of Carlo Nasisse.*

Pricillia. Mixed media, hydrocal, epoxy, and found objects,
45" x 18" x 20", 2010. *Courtesy of Carlo Nasisse.*

Dolly. Mixed media, hydrocal, epoxy, and found objects,
33" x 42" x 12", 2008. *Courtesy of Carlo Nasisse.*

Courtney Garrett

I have a simple curiosity about the southern rural vernacular; call it homage if you will, or a reckoning of my brief homeland, but in any case I feel these landscapes are monumental to the retrospective recordings of our culture.

The land is changing, the people are changing, and somewhere in the imagery of my work, I see a humble recording of the overlooked. I am not a historian, but have had the common privilege to observe and the uncommon privilege to record a land and its evolution. It's a simple record of a simple land.

Yet within these uncomplicated pictures resides most of our senses. We can hear them, we feel them, and we understand them — because we've lived them. Particular bodies of work consist of images that have been changed by time and element or have even ceased to exist among the landscape. From an earlier series titled *Monuments and Movements*, I was able experiment with the idea that rural pictorial references were universally recognized crossed culturally, similar to the purpose and position of a national monument.

It's all about orchestrating an intimate moment between a painting and its observer. Through layering images, simple horizon lines, and even the manipulation of resin, my messaging and style remain hauntingly hopeful. There is a place in each of us where images reside as a recording of what we know. These images are mine.

Courtesy of Manda Faye Dunigan.

A Resurrection of Time Indefinite No. 1. Mixed media oil with resin on birch, 48" x 60", 2010.

Reckoning of My Homeland. Mixed media oil with resin on birch, 48" x 48," 2011.

Reconciliation No. 4. Mixed media oil with resin on birch. 24" x 24." 2011.

The Little Foxes Turned and the Fields Stopped Bleeding No. 14.
Mixed media oil with resin on birch, 48" x 48", 2011.

Waiting in the Water No. 5.
Mixed media oil with resin on
birch, 48" x 48", 2011.

Jennifer J L Jones

The things that inspire me to create are found all around me — in the seasons, weather patterns, and natural elements. The grace in a falling leaf from a tree in autumn, a pocket of air trapped in ice, the burnt edges on a flower in the hot summer, millions of crushed shells in the form of sand along the beach, southern oaks caressed with the romance of Spanish moss. The inspiration found in nature for my art seems endless. Beauty is everywhere, and as an artist I interpret that beauty, integrate my personal style, and put it out there for people to connect with.

As I paint, each studio session becomes a form of meditation. My work is an intuitive process. The paint often dictates the final imagery, and I allow this to be my guide. The colors I choose to glaze over one another create mood, atmosphere, and a "vibration" of energy unique to each viewer interacting with the final piece. Working with the paint and the various mediums and materials helps to build up and break down ideas, thoughts, and patterns. I believe that the process I follow when creating a new piece is just as important as the end result.

My paintings are my love songs, poems, and novels. They are my mysteries, questions, and answers. They are even my confusion, heartbreaks, and bliss. Through painting, I have discovered a visual voice for my heart that has evolved in to a serenade for my soul. My work is a synthesis representing the profound path of self-discovery and growth I experience every day and view as a continuing revelation and manifestation of my muse. My intent is that the positive energy conveyed through my paintings will be felt and promulgated by all who see and experience them.

Courtesy of Cameron Krone.

Flight of the Bees I. Mixed media painting on wood, 48" x 36", 2011. *Courtesy of Robert Hill.*

Sera. Mixed media painting on wood, 60" x 48", 2011.
Courtesy of Robert V. Hill.

Abundance. Mixed media painting on wood, 48" x 72", 2011.
Courtesy of Robert V. Hill.

Prelude to Spring. Mixed media painting on wood, 40" x 40," 2011.
Courtesy of Robert V. Hill.

Samsara. Mixed media painting on wood, 60" x 60", 2010.
Courtesy of Robert V. Hill.

David J. Kaminsky

After my wife, artist Betsy Cain, and I moved to Savannah, we were lucky enough to find a home on the edge of the marsh, directly facing the barrier islands which protect the mainland from the force of the ocean. The tidal marsh is an environment that richly rewards all the senses in constantly changing light, sound, smell, and motion. It also presents a wide panoramic view for miles that is a distinct change from the densely forested landscape that makes up a large part of the state.

The works included here were the answer to a challenge I gave myself to create images that captured the feel and ambiance of the marsh and ultimately other subjects, with the smallest amount of information possible, while still being visually engaging. In starting with only one pixel of data in one plane and expanding that in a linear manner, the images work on different levels when seen from different distances. From a distance, there is the recognition of the subject. At a medium distance, there is actually a point where visual uncertainty is created with the eyes unable to focus properly, being confused by the very fine lines that make up the image. Then at a close range the pure abstract beauty of the seemingly random color combinations becomes paramount.

I've always been fascinated by the Surrealist's "automatic drawing" technique. Creating a complete image from a tiny, tiny bit of true but also ultimately random information is my personal homage to that idea.

Courtesy of Jan Clayton Pagratis.

Ossabaw #1. Pigment ink on canvas, 30" x 60", Limited edition of 50 © 2010.

Flowering Kale at Sunrise. Pigment ink on canvas,
40" x 60", Limited edition of 50 © 2011.

Self Portrait. Pigment ink on canvas, 30" x 30",
Limited edition of 50 © 2010.

Tom's Creek #1. Pigment ink on canvas, 40" x 60", Limited edition of 50 © 2010.

Marcus Kenney

Oh to make Art… To call it Art, to sell it Art, to eat it Art, to treat it Art, to beat it Art, and to sex it Art. To hate it! To love it! To run from it Art! To cry about it! To buy it! To try it Art! To kill it! To steal it! To will it Art. To believe it! To deceive it! To retrieve it Art. Oh to make Art!

The New Communism. Reclaimed taxidermy, human hair, various twines, chain mail, gold leaf, leather, aluminum wire, nuts, bolts, panty hose, etc., 21" x 20" x 11", 2008. *Courtesy of Imke Lass.*

Almighty. Wooden head, shrub, currency, photographs, marker, cigarette paper, medallion, tennis shoes, organic materials, baby doll parts, darts, nails, screws, twine, thread, cigar labels, wax, bones, hooks, incense sticks, and other miscellaneous objects, 35" x 78" x 28", 2010. *Courtesy of Imke Lass.*

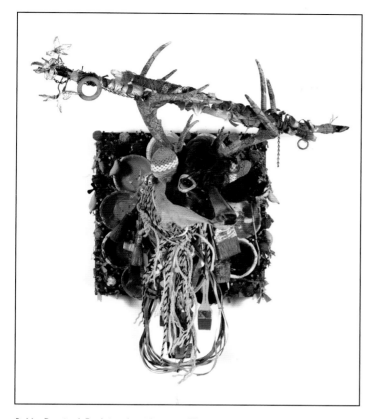

Bubba Demigod. Reclaimed taxidermy, rubber, various ropes, oil, paper bowls, nails, paint brushes, beads, sticks, various fabrics, mediums, glazes on panel, 44" x 38" x 30", 2010. *Courtesy of Imke Lass.*

Natcheketi. Reclaimed taxidermy, fabric, wig, rope, fur, beads, buttons, and miscellaneous objects on panel, 24" x 39" x 20", 2010. *Courtesy of Imke Lass.*

KicKitic. Reclaimed taxidermy, fabric, gar, felt, turtle shell, beads, twine, buttons, plastic, miscellaneous objects on panel, 36" x 38" x 25", 2010. *Courtesy of Imke Lass.*

Christy Kinard

In *Life on the Mississippi*, Mark Twain writes, "A Southerner talks music."

If a Southerner talks music, weaving symphonies of vibrant wordplay, I would like to think that I paint similarly, creating rich compositions with impressions of southern life. The abundant flowers and unique cultural traditions of the South sing through me, into my hands and onto the materials that shape my visual song. I attempt to capture the joyful, layered character of the South, working from both childhood memories and life.

Flowers are the main subjects of my work, which reflects the bounty of colorful plant life both outside and in the homes of the South. To represent these bouquets, I created my own visual language partially inspired by the southern quilting tradition. Instead of picking up a needle, however, I picked up a paintbrush to paint and collage layers of patterns and textures with simplified bold shapes and weaving lines.

The boldness of my work can also be related to the southern character. To be southern is to be happy and laid back, to say hello to strangers who you pass on the street, and to spend time sitting on the porch enjoying the simple beauty that nature provides.

Courtesy of Aharon Hill Photography.

Porch Hydrangea. Mixed media, 30" x 40".
Courtesy of Aharon Hill Photography.

Patchwork Flowers. Mixed media, 48" x 48".
Courtesy of Aharon Hill Photography.

Mixed Bouquet. Mixed media, 40" x 30".
Courtesy of Aharon Hill Photography.

Gifts of the Spirit. Mixed media, 40" x 30".
Courtesy of Aharon Hill Photography.

Neighbors. Mixed media, 24" x 24". *Courtesy of Aharon Hill Photography.*

Yellow Rose II. Mixed media, 36" x 36". *Courtesy of Aharon Hill Photography.*

Tracey Lane

My work is about the experience of light and shadow, color and texture, the play between the seen and the unseen, between memory and imagination. I am most inspired by the quiet drama of nature: trees bending toward the light, silent reflections, sunlight breaking through clouds. Whether it's memories of childhood summers spent on Jekyll Island, Georgia, where live oaks drip Spanish moss, or of time spent riding my horse as a young girl, or the many years that I've spent exploring the fourteen-acre forest where my mother still lives today, a deep connection to the earth and trees in particular was part of me long before I started painting.

I work on wood panels because the surface can withstand both the weight of the texture and the force and briskness with which I apply paint: sometimes using brushes and other times palette knives, combining heavy, thickly applied paint with watery washes that drip randomly. This process enables me to capture the spirit of the subject, its wildness. For wildness, as Bill McKibben writes in *The End of Nature*, stirs the imagination and creates in us "the sense that we are part of something with roots stretching back nearly forever, and branches reaching forward just as far."

©Digital Sidekicks 2011.

Three Graces. Acrylic on panels, 15" x 45" ea., 2008.

Hombre. Acrylic on panel, 45" x 24", 2010.

Life as a Tree. Acrylic on panel, 40" x 50", 2010.

Like a River to the Vast Sea. Acrylic on panel, 40" x 40", 2010.

Sparrow. Acrylic on panel, 20" x 20", 2011.

Bring to Light. Acrylic on panel, 36" x 36", 2011.

Jeffrey Lange

The South to me is the richness of its changing flora interwoven with the contrast of its seasons to create an ever-changing palette of tones that permeate my work. I love the temperament of the South with its warmth of climate and people that instills a sense of comfort and tranquility. The timeless beauty of the South, steeped in historical significance, creates an allure that is unique to this wonderful region.

I like to build layers of paint and collage in a non-thinking approach and then keep or destroy an image to arrive at a point that is based on chaos. I like to create with destruction and chaos.

Anatomical. Mixed media, 60" x 72", 2010. *Courtesy of Susan Lange.*

Aloof. Mixed media, 24" x 24", 2010. *Courtesy of Susan Lange.*

Room with a View I. Mixed media, 15" x 15", 2009. *Courtesy of Susan Lange.*

Ways and Means. Mixed media, 35" x 30", 2011. *Courtesy of Susan Lange.*

Room with a View II. Mixed media, 15" x 15", 2009. *Courtesy of Susan Lange.*

Ruth Laxon

On being an artist in the space of Southland USA… First, you sharpen the tools and banish fear of dirt. If you need other tools, first try to make, forge, or trade them. Now nurture love of work. No problem because I grew up on a farm and inherited the resourcefulness of two exemplary creative parents. This prologue sets the stage for the labor intensiveness of my art — the cutting, gouging, typesetting, inking, on and on.

From the beginning, my art showed traces of markings as cryptic language. (In first grade, I thought of the alphabet as little pictures.) The art started as drawings on gesso board, next large color wood cut prints. My encounter with handmade paper in the late '70s almost led me astray because the pieces were collected for decorative uses, but this short phase put me in touch with the network for artists, books — the presses, artists, critics, scholars, collectors, etc. So my studio soon became Press 63+, and my work took on real credibility. The books drew attention from major collectors like museum and university libraries in the country and elsewhere and many in the private sector.

The books were done by typography, etching with aquatint and chine colle, embossing, drawing, and offset. The editions varied in size from 10 to 200, except for two offset editions of 500 each. The bindings are mostly hand done by me.

The facility for the use of language was embedded deep inside, and I assumed the authority to harness it in a playful and pithy way. It became visual and concrete poetry with automatic writing and stream of consciousness commentary weaving within shapes. There is evidence I have unwittingly listened well.

An ongoing series of drawings that I call god dolls have been a big feature of my work starting around 1996. They are about the ways we play with God and other political issues.

Just A Note. Copper plate etching, with hard ground, aquatint, and chine colle, 15" x 18", 2009. *Courtesy of Kathy Garrou.*

Ideas of God. Handset type on Challenger flatbed press, drawings, 38-page, black hardbound cover, 8.5" x 11", 2008. *Courtesy of Digital Sidekicks.*

Brave Girl. Ink, gouache on Murillo paper, 27.5" x 19.5", 2008. *Courtesy of Digital Sidekicks.*

Guru. Ink, gouache on Murillo paper, 27.5" x 19.5", 2007. *Courtesy of Digital Sidekicks.*

A Hundred Years of LEX FLEX (pp. 21-22). Typography, offset printed on Heidelberg press, hardbound cover, 8.5" x 11", 2003. *Courtesy of Digital Sidekicks.*

Alan Loehle

My work recently underwent a significant change. Prior to 2008, I tended to invest a single dominant image in the painting (a dog, meat, a man with achondroplasia) with all of the emotional weight and meaning. My intent was to prompt a sense of pathos on the part of the viewer: a recognition of our own vulnerabilities. The "Liminal Dog" paintings are part of this series; the dogs inhabit space in psychically charged ways, an embodiment of our own corporeality and struggles as human beings.

In 2008, I went to Rome on a Guggenheim Fellowship with the intent of developing ideas for new work. The paintings that resulted were stylistically and thematically very different, juxtaposing cultural symbols, images from art history, and myriad other sources through a process of cognitive free association. However different in appearance these new paintings are, the overriding concern in each is still with addressing the human condition. The paintings are meant to create an echo chamber of associations and connections for the viewer — for the self and other, now and the past, our hopes and fears. They are an attempt to make sense of experience, to capture the bigness of being alive in the world, to somehow tickle the back corners of the viewer's mind and spirit. Each in its own way is an attempt to distill the world and get everything organized in one place. They are an acknowledgement of both tragedy and beauty.

I have lived in the South off and on for many years. I came here as a teenager and still view it somewhat as an outsider. Yet the fecundity, the light, a sense of time that exists here in the South has become a strong part of the work.

Liminal Dog I. Oil on canvas, 63" x 50", 2007.
Courtesy of Michael McKelvey.

Liminal Dog IV. Oil on canvas, 45" x 49", 2007.
Courtesy of Michael McKelvey.

Sistine Lust. Oil on canvas, 51" x 37-3/4", 2010.
Courtesy of Michael McKelvey.

Chaos I. Oil and paint stick on canvas, 45-1/4" x 34-1/4", 2010.
Courtesy of Michael McKelvey.

Rome Dog. Oil and paint stick on canvas, 49" x 38-1/2", 2010.
Courtesy of Michael McKelvey.

Philip Morsberger

Color color color!
Color as music.
Color as narrative.
Color as prayer.
And yes...color as laughter!

Having spent long years in Oxford, England, and in Berkeley, California, I feel, having grown up in Maryland, that by moving to Georgia, I have come full circle, being back once more in the American Southeast where it all began. T. S. Eliot put it nicely: "We shall not cease from exploration; and the end of all our exploring will be to arrive at where we started and know the place for the first time."

Eliot was writing about the making of art, but the making of art cannot be separated from the input — the ambience — of the place where the art is being made, and I like the quiet support and respect for privacy that I feel artists are given here.

Courtesy of Ashleigh Burke Coleman.

Epiphany (No. 3). Oil on canvas, 68-1/2" x 60-1/2", 1996-2005.
Courtesy of Ashleigh Burke Coleman.

Contradictions. Oil on canvas, 68" x 42", 1998-2008.
Courtesy of Ashleigh Burke Coleman.

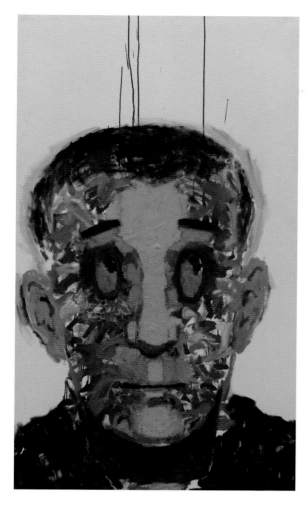

Man Reflecting. Oil on canvas, 69" x 40", 1999-2006.
Courtesy of Ashleigh Burke Coleman.

Fathers and Sons (No. 2). Oil on canvas, 68" x 38-1/2", 2005.
Courtesy of Ashleigh Burke Coleman.

Epiphany. Oil on canvas, 68" x 48", 1992-2000.
Courtesy of Ashleigh Burke Coleman.

Barbara Olsen

I grew up listening to tales of mischievous fairies and leprechauns told to me by my Irish immigrant father. It is only natural that I continue along this path. Incorporating snippets of fabric, found papers, wise and whimsical sayings are an important part of the stories I am telling with paint and canvas.

I have been blessed with a playful spirit and the gift of creating work that makes people smile; I could hardly ask for more. I am a self-taught artist, and painting is a never-ending learning process. Each day I look toward continuing work on a piece I have already begun or to beginning a new painting. I am compulsive in my need to create, and each day is a new experience with texture, color, and sometimes frustration when the emotion I am feeling and wanting to convey is eluding me. Then when the colors and shapes all come together, a real sense of accomplishment surrounds me.

I am a Northern California transplant to Georgia. Living in the South has provided me with a whole new vocabulary of images that represent the world around me. Southern living is lush with scenic beauty, history, sounds, and hospitality.

Courtesy of John Olsen.

Opposites Attract. Mixed media on canvas, 20" x 20". *Courtesy of Anne Irwin Fine Art.*

Stand by Your Pan. Mixed media on canvas, 36" x 24". *Courtesy of Anne Irwin Fine Art.*

I Want the Apple. Mixed media on canvas, 30" x 30". *Courtesy of Anne Irwin Fine Art.*

Giddy Up. Mixed media on canvas, 24" x 24".
Courtesy of Anne Irwin Fine Art.

The Hammer Man. Mixed media on canvas, 18" x 24".
Courtesy of Anne Irwin Fine Art.

Jan Clayton Pagratis

My paintings are filled with ideas, memories, and fragments of experiences associated with growing up and living on the southeastern coast of the United States. I was born in Miami, Florida, and grew up playing on warm beaches with white sand and horseshoe crabs. My move to Savannah, Georgia, about fifteen years ago inspired a series of plein air works that had me painting in marshes, on beaches, under bridges, and in the historic squares of downtown. Being outside in the elements, I soaked up the environment with enthusiasm. Over the past four or five years, I've moved back to painting in the studio, which has allowed me to create larger canvases but more importantly has allowed me to contemplate that which inspires me.

The subject for these recent works is that of abstracted imagery, often sparked by a particular event or moment in time; thus, the content is created by the emotional tone that surrounds each memory. I hope to capture the shimmer of reflected light on dancing leaves, or tangled grasses at the edge of a marsh, or blue rain mixed with sunshine. Each painting is dense with multiple layers of transparent oil paint and imbued with multiple layers of experiences. Another important aspect of my studio practice is to play around with my collection of discarded matter and recycled materials. For years I have saved paint scrapings from my palette; once I have enough paint, I am able to create a bricolage. I'm interested in working with the different media, often juxtaposing and building surface textures with paint, wax, rusted metal, found objects, and other oddities.

Artist with *A Man Walking His Blue Dog with Sunshine on His Shoulder*. Courtesy of Janae Minor.

All the Kings Horses and All the Kings Men of Corfu. Oil on canvas, 40" x 30", 2009.

Beyond the Yellow Grasses Lies the Blue Water. Oil on canvas, 48" x 48", 2009.

The Seasons: Vivaldi's Spring. Oil on canvas, 48" x 36", 2008.
Courtesy of David Kaminsky.

The Seasons: Vivaldi's Summer. Oil on canvas, 48" x 36", 2008.
Courtesy of David Kaminsky.

Sweet Shimmer. Oil on canvas, 24" x 36", 2008.

Susie Pryor

Born and raised in Athens, Georgia, I have been painting all my life and it is an integral part of my being. I suppose in some way I am narrating my perception of life and nature through paint. My objective is to give life and emotion to subject matter that is visually gripping and exciting. Exploration and experimentation are at the core of my process. This inherent stimulation of discovery keeps me challenged to explore the endless possibilities of painting. The work is a dialog of light and shadow followed by the incorporation of opaque textures and transparent layers. While various subjects come into play, the completely uninhibited way that children approach each moment often sparks the fire that drives me to paint. Each painting involves an exciting struggle between abstraction and reality. I prefer to minimally represent a form or subject and allow the paint to bring the form into a life of its own. The real highs of painting, however, are derived from achieving a balance between control and spontaneity. Inspiration only happens when I connect with an image. What follows is an overwhelming need to express the connection through paint. The connections are sometimes images in the southern landscape that take me back to a time and place where I understood the world though the eyes of a child. I am celebrating the purity and beauty of simple subjects like children, old barns, trees, and flowers through paint; it is exhilarating.

Dressed in Magic. Oil, 60" x 48", 2009. Courtesy of Ginger Ann Clark.

Dancing in Blue. Oil, 48" x 48", 2006. Courtesy of Ginger Ann Clark.

Beach Towel. Oil, 48" x 60", 2010. Courtesy of Ginger Ann Clark.

Path. Oil, 72" x 48", 2009. Courtesy of Ginger Ann Clark.

Make a Wish. Oil, 60" x 48", 2010.
Courtesy of Ginger Ann Clark.

Morgan Santander

Having lived, worked, and taught in Savannah over the last eleven years has contributed greatly to my artistic direction and view of the world. The South hosts a wealth of visual, historical, and cultural material. Artists of all kinds have a lot to draw from living in this region. Savannah's rich history and diversity of population make it a stimulating place to produce art and engage a diverse community. A large portion of my work is initially produced subconsciously. Meaning becomes layered though rich veils of color, iconography, and energetic application of paint. The work becomes symbolically encoded through the painting process. My work is always saturated with art/historical symbolism referencing a wide range of interests.

Artist with untitled oil painting, 2009.

Free bird. Acrylic on canvas, 84" x 94", 2011.

Red Sculpture Garden #2. Oil on canvas, 24" x 36", 2009.

Morning of Carnaval. Acrylic on panel, 25" x 49", 2011.

Red Sculpture Garden. Oil on canvas, 165" x 94", 2000.

Kim Schuessler

Having been born and raised in Georgia, my southern roots run deep and for this I am grateful. As with most Southerners, my faith is strong, my family comes first, and I'm passionate about my work. The world has many distractions and choices, but I define success as staying focused on the few things that are truly important.

My work represents the importance of having people in our lives and of understanding the universal proverbs of this world. Although I have traveled and studied in many places around the globe, I find that, although the scenery changes, much remains the same. For example, we all need someone to love and something to hope for. My paintings depict these common essentials as I illustrate couples dancing, families celebrating, and friends standing together.

Visually, I am inspired by colors, patterns, fashion, and spatial relationships. To date, my greatest sense of accomplishment has been seeing people enjoy my works at places I never imagined: The Hank Aaron Museum, the Atlanta Botanical Gardens, and in periodicals such as *Pink* and *Better Homes and Gardens*. I am an optimist who wants my audience to pursue their passion, to find joy in everyday occurrences and to cherish those they love.

Courtesy of Tracy Adams.

Dressed in a promise of a rainbow. Mixed media, 48" x 36". *Courtesy of Tracy Adams.*

Find your support. Mixed media, 48" x 36". Courtesy of Tracy Adams.

Sowing seeds of love. Mixed media, 36" x 48".
Courtesy of Tracy Adams.

United we stand. Mixed media, 60" x 48". Courtesy of Tracy Adams.

Socially responsible. Mixed media, 24" x 48".
Courtesy of Tracy Adams.

Katherine Taylor

I grew up in Biloxi, Mississippi, near the Gulf of Mexico, where the natural environment engenders both destructive and revitalizing forces. Because of this, I often think of the southern landscape as a state of mind, shaped by memories and experience, a real and fantastical place framing many perspectives of the South.

I now live and work in Atlanta, Georgia. Although I focus on popular familiar images from the media, photographs, and public records, my paintings depict universal cause and effect in an unstable relationship with the natural world. Unpopulated beautiful views represent destructive forces, and resurgent vistas embody destruction.

The lens through which we see the world shapes our popular view. As such, the reoccurring themes of devastation and resurrection are components of how I read a fixed image. For the receptive viewer, my paintings are silent mediations of these signs and symbols.

Oasis-Indexical View/Sabal Palm. Oil on canvas, 60" x 48", 2009. *Courtesy of Reis Birdwhistell.*

Grand Prix. Oil on canvas, 72" x 108", 2006. *Courtesy of Reis Birdwhistell.*

Projected Ruin. Charcoal and ink on paper, 78" x 84", 2010.
Courtesy of Reis Birdwhistell.

Oasis-Fantastical View/ Waterfront Lot. Oil on canvas, 60" x 48", 2009.
Courtesy of Reis Birdwhistell.

Marine. Oil on canvas, 72" x 108", 2009. *Courtesy of Reis Birdwhistell.*

W. Gerome Temple

I have been working in Savannah, Georgia, as an illustrator for more than fifteen years. Inspired by a lifetime fascination with natural history and bookplate etchings, I begin my "Fictional Entomologies" with an in-depth study of living insects that come to visit my garden. With this observational foundation, I create fictional forms of discovered life. I explore ideas of flight in my Air & Atmosphere Club series. Inspiration comes from imagining the time when flight was still a mystery, and many were experimenting with form and function while seeking personal notoriety — just as the Wright Brothers first explored flight on the coast of North Carolina. The rambling architectural gems of historic Savannah consistently absorb me. In my "Antiquity & Technology" illustrations, these architectural features are incorporated into drawings that depict a world where antiquity meets crude but futuristic technology. Savannahians are gifted at finding any reason to come together for revelry. My circus drawings are infused with this light-hearted mind-set, cast against the architectural pillars found in historic Savannah.

Perpetual Machine Giantique. Pigment and ink on Bristol paper, 7.5" x 24", 2008.

Omnia Vincit Amor. Pigment and ink on Bristol paper, 9.5" x 5.5", 2009.

Hartford with His Stationary Dictator of Word. Pigment and ink on Bristol paper, 7" x 6.25", 2009.

North Lachaum Lightning's. Pigment and ink on Bristol paper, 8" x 10.5", 2010.

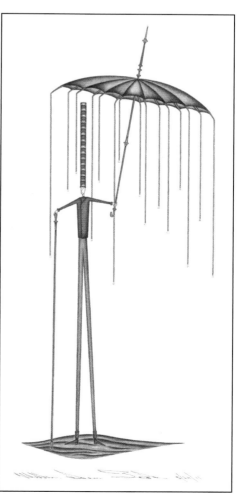

Tall Man In The Rain. Pigment and ink on Bristol paper, 13" x 5", 2011.

Dayna Thacker

My work embodies a long-standing interest in how our inner and outer selves interact, inform, and create each other: physical and spiritual, logical and intuitive, intellectual and psychological, conscious and subconscious. We create our selves, which create the world, which alters and recreates our selves. I think of it as the never-ending shaping of the modern soul. If our bodies are what we eat, then it stands to reason that our souls, or at least our psychological selves, are what we think and feel. Modern-day stresses, emotional represses, the vast amounts of information we must process daily, all contribute to the ramshackle hodgepodge of the contemporary self. Our creations aren't perfect: we throw things together, we make-do, we invent ways of coping, we wedge in a few moments of joy, and then we let our subconscious devise an explanation that loosely holds it all together.

I don't consider my work to be particularly "southern," but I think the tolerance for eccentricity in the South, paired with the corresponding fondness for a good story and dark humor, has certainly influenced my work.

In your own words. Collaged paper, graphite, pastel on panel, 22" x 18", 2010.

Knee deep in my own brilliance. Collaged paper and altered photograph, graphite on paper, 4.75" x 6.75", 2011.

Kids these days. Collaged paper and altered photograph, graphite on paper, 6.75" x 4.75", 2010.

Implied agreement by tenant. Collaged paper, graphite, pastel on panel, 48" x 60", 2010.

Nothing never mind. Collaged paper, graphite, acrylic paint on panel, 29" x 27", 2010.

The quantity of things. Collaged paper, graphite, acrylic paint on panel, 15" x 14", 2010.

Matt Toole

I grew up playing in the woods around the barrier islands and salt marshes of Savannah, Georgia. This is where I came to embrace the beauty and imperfection of the natural world, in particular the large live oaks that are some of the Low Country's greatest attributes. I have always been interested in dynamic forms shaped by environmental forces over time, where the evidence of tension and strain lends to their beauty. Like a smooth stone that has worked its way down a river over many years or the gnarled and twisted branches that have struggled to seek light over decades, these objects beckon to be observed more closely. Through a number of fellowships and awards, I have been fortunate to be afforded many opportunities to create this work around the United States and the United Kingdom.

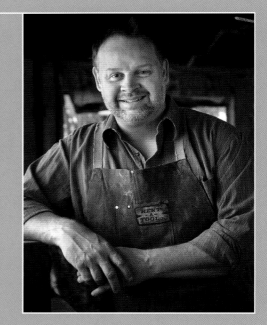

I am also a consummate collector of unique items, like old machines and knickknacks. My intention in marrying the organic materials with the functional objects is to commemorate the allure of their contrasting aesthetics. Breaking free of static, austere compositions, I favor dynamic or kinetic arrangements to further reference the element of time. My interest in the transformation of materials has led to a series of performance events that highlight the moment when a work of art is created. Focusing on the process of casting iron, my performances serve not only as a means to create objects but to mark points in time, thus connecting the resulting artwork to the immediate act. Most often the event is a tribute to the rite of creative expression, focusing on the power of a collective experience rather than that of an individual artist acting alone to create. In these performances, the structures used to melt, pour, and receive the molten metal essentially function as artworks that create other works of art, utilizing fire as a means of devastation while simultaneously employing it as an instrument of origination.

Circularis. Kinetic Sculpture made of found objects, mahogany, steel, copper, and bone, 16" x 33" x 9", 2008.

Chosen. Found objects, wood, iron, nut, 13" x 5" x 4", 2010. *Courtesy of George Gill.*

Dipper. Kinetic Sculpture made of found objects, mahogany, pecan, steel, copper, 28" x 36" x 10", 2007. *Courtesy of Imke Lass.*

Kinship: A Tribute of Iron. Performance Event, 6th International Conference on Contemporary Cast Iron Art, Kidwelly, Wales, United Kingdom; various materials and dimensions, 2010.

Fire Performance: Law of Unintended Consequences. Performance Event, Georgia Southern University, Statesboro, Georgia; various materials and dimensions, 2006. *Courtesy of David Caselli.*

Rise of the Vulcanites: Phase II, Indulgence. Performance Event, Franconia Sculpture Park, Shafer, Minnesota; various materials and dimensions, 2002. *Courtesy of Dick Sonnen.*

4.
North Carolina

Gary Bills

My love for woodturning was first ignited in 1962. As a young Michigan student, I turned two bowls on a wood lathe in my high school shop class. There and then I promised myself I would get back to woodturning — once I got my life, work, and family under way. It took forty-one years to keep that promise to myself.

In 2003, after retiring from Dow Chemical (Michigan) and moving to the breathtaking Blue Ridge Mountains of Zirconia, North Carolina, I took a woodturning class, bought a Powermatic 3520a wood lathe, and a 17-inch Grizzly band saw and started turning wood. As my expertise grew, so did the size of my pieces and the enthusiasm I felt when bringing into focus the unique features locked within each piece of wood. That has become the focus of my work; creating a one-of-a-kind-piece that spotlights the unique character found within the wood — wood that grows all around me here in the mountains. Another aspect of the woodturning process that I find exciting is "the hunt!" I love working with local green wood and spend lots of time traveling country roads in search of unusual trees that have fallen during a storm or felled by disease. Often, trees under stress develop internal patterns or "markings" in their grain that can be the focus of the art piece I am creating.

My earlier hobby of collecting antique glassware has helped develop my understanding of shapes and forms that best please the eye. This training has served me well in developing the sensuous curves that are the basis for all of my pieces. It is a thrill watching a piece of wood come to life as the beauty in the grain is uncovered and showcased by the shape or form I have created.

Artist with his woodturning art.

The Underground. Wood: eastern hop hornbeam, 9" x 10", 2009.

Jack-O-Lantern. Wood: sycamore, 16" x 16", 2004.

More or Less. Wood: sycamore, 15" x 13", 2004.

Spokes. Wood: Norfolk Island pine, 5-1/2" x 6-1/2", 2008.

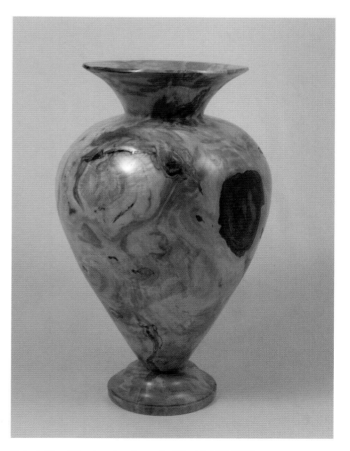

Metropolitan. Wood: ambrosia maple, 7" x 11-1/2", 2009.

Ashlynn Browning

My work is about creating a hybrid of calculated and intuitive painting processes. The goal is for a finished painting to incorporate structure and accident, restraint and recklessness, deliberation and instinct. In these paintings, geometric forms function as stand-ins for places and more often for figures, each with its own body language, mood, and narrative. Some are bold and upright, others hesitant, crouching, and precarious. The awkward tension inherent in these postures reflects different sides of myself.

Experimenting with the idea of opposing forces is also a large factor in this series. Bold color against muted, geometric forms mixing with organic, painterly texture against flat planes, pattern against color field — these are variables that I mix, layer, and wipe away in multiple stages until a resonant image is formed. There is always an attempt to strike balance.

Living in the South is also an issue of balance for me. Growing up in Charlotte, North Carolina, and living now in Raleigh, North Carolina, I have always had equal measures of city life along with easy access to the mountains and coast. This approach works well for me, providing both the practical, urban things I need as an artist along with the more spiritual aspects that come with outdoor life, changing seasons, and room to roam and garden. Raleigh is a city that honors tradition and history but at the same time is home to cultural diversity, offering all the elements of a more metropolitan area. I enjoy basing my life and art career here, while being able to exhibit locally and nationally.

Hot and Pink. Oil on panel, 14" x 11", 2010. *Courtesy of David Bibb*.

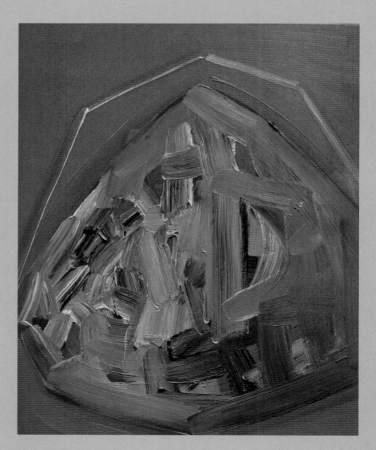

Light in the Heart of the Jungle. Oil on panel, 20" x 16", 2010.
Courtesy of David Bibb.

Bound. Oil on panel, 20" x 16", 2010.
Courtesy of David Bibb.

Braced. Oil on panel, 20" x 20", 2010.
Courtesy of David Bibb.

Containing Energies. Oil on panel, 18" x 18", 2010.
Courtesy of David Bibb.

Loren DiBenedetto

Growing up, my parents always told me, "You can do anything you want if you put your mind to it." These wise words gave me the confidence to pursue a career in art. Upon entering art school, I recall one instructor telling me and the other students that, if we didn't have the "right stuff" now, we never would. And he made it clear to me that he thought I lacked the necessary talent. Well, from then on, I was dead set on proving him wrong. His less-than-encouraging words stoked my sense of determination and helped me become a better artist.

Once I had my classical training behind me, it was time to chart my own artistic course. About this time, my husband and I relocated from the Northeast to the South for a warmer, sunnier climate along with a more relaxed way of life. With this new "southern lifestyle," my goal was to slow down and focus on my art. But what to paint? That was probably the one thing I struggled with most. Finally, after years of painting what I thought people would like to see, I had an epiphany. I read an article in an artist's magazine that said "paint what you know." From the age of thirteen through adulthood, I had worked in the floral industry as a designer. I had always loved flowers and gardening and all things to do with nature. So my artistic inspiration had been right in front of me the whole time. At that point, I started painting large floral pieces, oversized fruits, and vegetables and never struggled with what to paint again. I paint every day and couldn't imagine doing anything else with my life.

Courtesy of Deborah Young Studio.

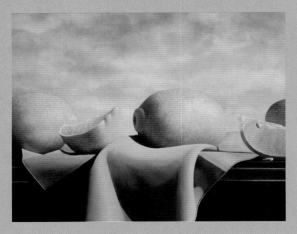

Lemons and sky. Oil on linen, 24" x 30", 2011.

Drying hydrangea. Oil on linen, 36" x 24", 2011.

Eggs and oak leaves. Oil on linen, 22" x 28", 2011.

Nest on branch. Oil on linen, 24" x 36", 2010.

Magnolias. Oil on linen, 20" x 20", 2011.

Three cherries. Oil on linen, 14" x 18", 2011.

Steven Forbes-DeSoule

To me, the South is more than just a geographic place on the map. It signals the birth of my career as an artist. After a grueling and unfulfilling career in the corporate world, I took stock of my life and decided to start over in a new location. My move to the South corresponded with the start of my art career and my journey as an artist. Today, when I work in my home studio, I have all the inspiration I need right outside my window, where the panoramic vistas of the Blue Ridge Mountains provide unlimited examples of color, texture, and shape.

It is no coincidence that the serendipity of the raku firing creates the spontaneous colors in my glazes, for the energy of raku matches the wild, unfettered energy of western North Carolina. This rugged landscape has remained untamed for centuries and is a gift for all who take the time to observe and appreciate its grandeur.

Inspiration is only part of the equation, however. In order to be fulfilled as an artist, one has to have an appreciative audience. I live near Asheville, North Carolina, a thriving city rated as one of the best small art markets in the US. For nearly one hundred years, this area has been known for its rich arts heritage. When I moved here, Asheville was just becoming a destination for collectors of fine craft and art. Now, galleries and studios make up a large portion of downtown Asheville, and visitors come daily to experience our thriving art scene.

Midnight Sun. Raku, 12" x 15", 2011.

Winged Vessel #1. Raku, 15" x 6" x 13", 2010.

Golden Sky. Raku, 16" x 12", 2010.

Valley Rain. Raku, 12" x 8", 2011.

Winged Vessel #2. Raku, 15" x 8" x 17", 2010.

Charlotte Foust

As the South continues to grow and change, I still hold close memories of hot summer days playing in the fields of rural North Carolina. My southern identity is an internal experience, and I still call North Carolina home. Born, raised, and currently maintaining my studio in Charlotte, I have a love and respect for nature and strong family ties to support my creative endeavors.

In an intuitive painting process, I am free to explore the depths of my imagination and creativity. A single mark or line on a blank surface provides a starting point for an exploration of the visual language found in abstract art. Working in acrylics allows me to paint with multiple layers and reworked surfaces — with each painting being a delightful discovery of things unseen. From the red clay of the Piedmont to the sandy shores of the coast, a unique southern style, full of charm and mystery always waits to be unearthed under the Carolina blue sky.

Artist with *High Altitudes*.

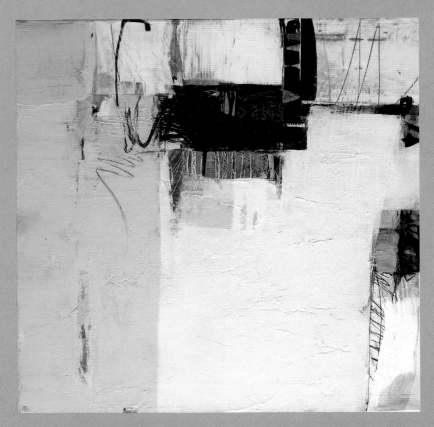

Aqua I. Mixed media on canvas, 24" x 24", 2010.

Aqua II. Mixed media on canvas, 24" x 24", 2010.

Barricade. Mixed media on canvas, 48" x 48", 2011.

Renewal. Mixed media on canvas, 48" x 60", 2010.

Skyscraper. Mixed media on canvas, 48" x 60", 2010.

George Handy

The title of my series, "Constructed Paintings," is a term borrowed from Matisse, who suggested "approach a painting as if you are constructing it."

My pallet is inspired by the gardens surrounding my Carolina mountain home. Bright and rich colors are often tucked along the edges while the dominant frontal surfaces are intentionally subdued; this relates to the brilliant, but small flower details and highlights the overall foliage of wildlife plants. My polygons are formed with fractal design, and Fibonacci sequence spirals are employed throughout the compositions, again reflecting the natural world and our Appalachian woodlands.

Frank Stella's "Exotic Birds" moved me. When he invited me to visit him in New York, a warm friendship began out of mutual respect for each other's work. My series of sculptures began after reading in Stella's book *Working Space* that Cubism never fully explored the possibilities of sculpture, but instead Picasso sped to renderings of the female figure. This "missed opportunity" offered an open space in history, prompting my studio focus. A show at the Bascom Art Center in Highlands, North Carolina, displayed both Stella's work and my own, revealing our working relationship. During the show I conducted a week-long workshop displaying my process and discussed Frank Stella's ideas.

My constructed paintings employ skewed perspective and complex angles; my paint is used to playfully imitate shadow; the result often creates a surprise. Additionally, my holographic-visual effect is a technique that invites interaction as it presents color-shifts when a viewer changes perspective.

Shown over the past thirty years in over fifty galleries, my work is included in the permanent collection of the Renwick Gallery of American Art of the Smithsonian Institute.

Courtesy of Tess Elizabeth Handy.

Arabesque. Wood and mixed media, 76" x 8" x 56", 2011.
Courtesy of Tim Barnwell, www.barnwellphoto.com.

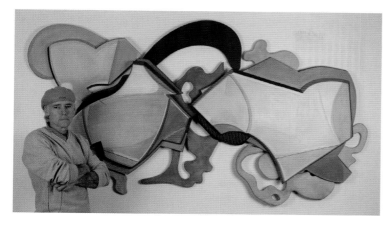

Constructed Painting #2. Wood and mixed media, 80" x 6" x 40". *Courtesy of David Humphreys Photography.*

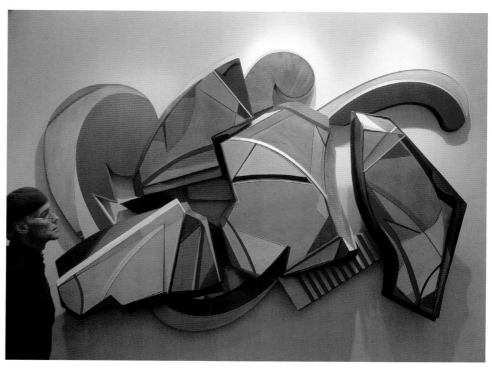

Shards. Wood and mixed media, 18" x 8" x 7". *Courtesy of Tim Barnwell, www.barnwellphoto.com.*

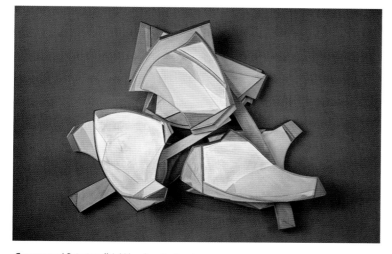

Constructed Painting #4. Wood and mixed media, 75" x 6" x 50". *Courtesy of David Humphreys Photography.*

Constructed Painting #3. Wood and mixed media, 70" x 9" x 42". *Courtesy of David Humphreys Photography.*

Ann Harwell

I was born in the mountains of North Carolina. I felt most at home among its great trees and flowers and underneath the thousands of stars visible in the clear night sky. My father and grandfather were Methodist ministers. I spent hours and hours in churches; my imagination ran wild as I stared at the stained glass windows during long sermons. Every little town we lived in had textile mills, fabric stores, and cotton fields. Sewing was a part of life, like cooking or cleaning, but to me it was special. My work is like stained glass made with cotton fabric. At first, I experimented with the symmetry of those windows, later finding inspiration in all of North Carolina's landscapes. The changing seasons in the mountains and the infinite shades of green, yellow, and orange; the hundred-year-old oaks and hundred-year-old houses scattered across the Piedmont; and the sunsets reflected off the sparkling oceans at our beaches are a constant source of color and beauty. To be inspired all I have to do is open my eyes, ears, and lungs.

Courtesy of Dick Cicone.

Colliding Spiral Galaxies. Cotton fabric pieced and quilted, 36" x 65", 2007.
Courtesy of Lynn Ruck.

Church in the Wildwood. Cotton fabric pieced and quilted, 65" x 71", 2003. *Courtesy of Lynn Ruck.*

Looking for Heaven on Earth. Cotton fabric pieced and quilted, 37" x 52", 2006. *Courtesy of Lynn Ruck.*

Bubble Nebula. Cotton fabric pieced and quilted. 51" x 53", 2001. *Courtesy of Lynn Ruck.*

Raleigh, City of Oaks. Cotton fabric pieced and quilted, 37" x 56", 2001. *Courtesy of Lynn Ruck.*

Geoffrey Johnson

Born in 1965 in Greensboro, North Carolina, I am a product of southern roots and cosmopolitan influence. Greensboro gained its wealth through tobacco and textiles, allowing the city to have some beautiful residences and modern factory buildings designed by notable architects. I took my sense of southern integrity and tradition from Greensboro to Philadelphia, where I received classical training at the Pennsylvania Academy of Fine Arts. During my time in Philadelphia, I spent many weekends traveling to New York to experience the movement, energy, and modernism of the city. In my first year of school, I was graciously awarded the first annual Campbell Soup Company Scholarship through a faculty jury — encouraging my artistic sensibilities. As my four years at PAFA continued, I found that my work began to coalesce into a combination of southern moodiness and urban expression. My fascination with the human figure and the powerful architecture of a modern city was commanding in my paintings. Returning to the South after school, I worked in Atlanta for several years and spent time visiting two of the most haunting southern cities: Savannah and Charleston. I was captivated by the interiors of several historic homes in both cities and began painting my own representations of these spaces. Just as in my cityscapes, I wanted to create a feeling of anonymity where figures became suggestive shapes and the line between abstraction and realism is captured. I came back to North Carolina several years ago and continue to experience the history, integrity, and character of the south.

Courtesy of Ali Ringenburg/Principle Gallery.

Untitled (Horses). Oil on panel, 16" x 24", 2010.
Courtesy of Ali Ringenburg/Principle Gallery.

Untitled. Oil on panel, 24" x 48", 2008.
Courtesy of Ali Ringenburg/Principle Gallery.

Study for Memorial. Oil on panel, 23" x 19", 2008.
Courtesy of Ali Ringenburg/Principle Gallery.

Study for Red Sofa. Oil on panel, 30" x 30", 2011.
Courtesy of Ali Ringenburg/Principle Gallery.

Forty People. Oil on canvas, 48" x 48", 2007.
Courtesy of Ali Ringenburg/Principle Gallery.

69th Street. Oil on panel, 20" x 16", 2009.
Courtesy of Ali Ringenburg/Principle Gallery.

Kenson (Marbut Thompson)

My artwork is the reflection of my journey through life with all its experiences and influences. Layers of paint and mixed media create a history, in time to be revealed and discovered through mistakes, surprises, and mysteries. I live in North Carolina surrounded by the natural world and am involved in a generous reflective environment. Southern music, writing, and poetry influence my process tremendously. Growing up in the South and raising two daughters has lent itself to magical explorations of this land as well as to the personal dynamics that friends and family offer. This has fostered an insatiable curiosity realized through my commitment and intention to resolve a continuous dialogue between the paint and me. Often what I see in my paintings is a surprise to me, offering inspiration to dig deep and uncover the gifts there to be discovered. Perhaps the emotional connection many viewers experience when looking at my work is made possible by some imaginative reality of personal stories and moments. I am deeply grateful for the vast and yet intimate silence present when I paint. My work is my life as I experience it, sharing my journey through this passion I love.

Proof of Cycles. Oil on canvas, 68" x 38", 2009.

Promise of Spring. Oil on board, 36" x 36", 2011.

In the Shadow of the Mountain. Mixed media on board, 24" x 32", 2011.

Poppy. Oil on board, 60" x 36", 2008.

Wishbone. Mixed media on board, 40" x 40", 2009.

Robert Levin

I was born and raised in Baltimore and have lived in North Carolina for thirty-six years. I moved to this area to teach at Penland School of Crafts in 1975 and then was the Resident Glass Artist for several years. Our children were born at Penland, and we still feel a strong connection to the school. We moved to our current home and studio in 1980. The mountains of western North Carolina are a beautiful area, home to many artists, fostering a sense of community and mutual support. The NC Arts Council has been very supportive of the artists in our state, and I have been fortunate to receive several NCAC grants and fellowships.

I was originally attracted to hot glass because of its liquid qualities and sense of immediacy. I try to capture the elegance, fluidity, and whimsy, which are inherent properties of glass. I make my own colored glasses and often frost the glass to emphasize the overall form of each piece. I find that various aspects of my work take on personal connotations for me. This usually does not happen consciously; I may be looking at a completed piece and see something new in it about my work or myself. This dialogue with the work has become very important to me. I view many of the pieces I've done as extensions of this dialogue and as analogies for my attempt to integrate the various facets of my life — the fusing of various parts, somewhat off-balance, but hopefully integrated into some sort of harmony. This all has something to do with possibilities for change and transformation, both with the material and with the person doing the creating. The approaches I use are eclectic and personal at the same time — sort of a blend of Late Venetian and Early Neurotic.

Red Splash Vessel. Hand-blown glass, 13.5"h, 2006.

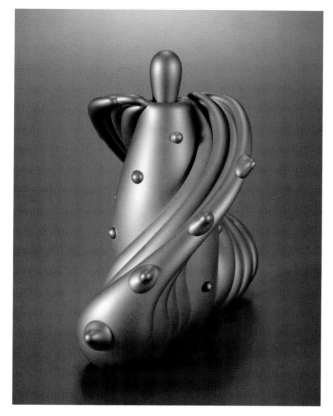

Caterpillar Bottle. Hand-blown glass, 5.75"h, 2006.

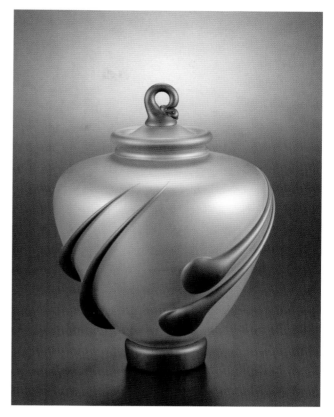

Urn. Hand-blown glass, 9.5"h, 2009.

Black Bumps #2. Hand-blown glass, 10"h, 2010.

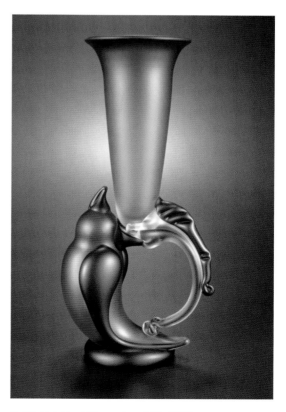

Bird Goblet. Hand-blown glass, 14"h, 2007.

Sandy Nelson

Growing up in the dark somber hills of eastern Kentucky, I painted landscapes of deep forests, creeks, and low light. When an opportunity to travel arose, I grabbed it with gusto. France, England and the desert southwest all showed up on my canvases. While all of that was artistically expanding and inspirational, it was not until I visited the South that I knew exactly how a landscape could pull you into its essence. A trip to the barrier islands of North Carolina in 1999 was revelatory. Marshes, wild maritime woods, seabirds, dunes and drifts, storms and calm, shifting light, and those dramatic skies were there in abundance. The romance and history of the place, the lure of the ocean, and live oaks dripping Spanish moss drew my paintbrush in. A year later, I moved to paint the southern coast. Thinking that I could explore the intricacies and moods of this place in a year — maybe two was laughable in retrospect. I've now been here for eleven years and only getting started.

Experience has taught me that to honestly express the beauty of a place, you must immerse yourself in it, explore its soul, and hope it loves your portrayal. From ever-changing light, to the intimate life of the marsh, this place holds eternal truths. I've stood on the edge of the marsh grass at dawn, breathing in the quiet, and felt reverence wash over me. It's as close to a spiritual awakening as I have come.

Courtesy of G. Frank Hart.

Wind Dancers II, 40" x 30", 2011.

Dawnlight, 24" x 30", 2011.

Queen Anne's Lace and Late Sun, 9" x 12", 2011.

Misty Marsh, 30" x 40", 2010.

Southern Skies, 30" x 40", 2010.

Keith Norval

Living in Raleigh, North Carolina, has had a big influence on my work for the past eleven years. I work in a studio located in a historic building in the downtown city market area. A graduate from the Savannah College of Art and Design in 2000, I moved to Raleigh. I wanted to stay in the South, but I also wanted to be closer to the mountains and the big cities of the Northeast.

My work incorporates a lot of personal symbols that relate to my background. Growing up in Zimbabwe, I always saw lots of wild animals. I use these African animals along with domestic animals and farm animals for the main subjects of my work. Personifying the animals gives them a whole new meaning to the context. I like putting a series of seemingly unrelated images together to create a new context for the whole.

My current series of quilted grid paintings examines the grid in a patchwork pattern inspired by quilts, comics, and city maps. Savannah got me interested in the city grid and the fabric of the city. Raleigh continues to feed my interest with a wealth of local history woven into its historic downtown. I am also interested in quilts and patterns created by repetition of certain elements.

Teaching also feeds my creativity, and I am constantly amazed by what my students create. I have been teaching painting, print-making, and sculpture in Raleigh since 2003. I have painted murals for various institutions and shown my work throughout the nation, but I am always the most excited about what I am currently working on.

Tusk. Oil on canvas, 16" x 20", 2011.

Black Owl Against Cubist Quilt. Oil on canvas, 18" x 36", 2011.

Big Daddy Owl II. Oil on canvas, 40" x 45", 2011.

Ladyfingers and Barracuda. Oil on canvas, 48" x 48", 2011.

Black Elephant. Oil on canvas, 20" x 22", 2010.

Wrong on Math Test. Oil on canvas, 48" x 60", 2008.

Janet Orselli

Growing up in the South, I've often experienced a sense of stopped time. Things seem to change slowly as if waiting for some magical moment of metamorphosis. At an early age, I felt that the old and worn had a great deal of meaning and was more valuable than the new. So when I began making art, I chose to live in the South and make art from leftovers of the past. I find my raw materials in dark spider-webby attic corners, inside boxes hidden in the basement, or in the junk pile down the street. Old baby carriages, bird's nests, crutches, turtle shells, roller skates, broken bits of the discarded stuff of everyday life are what I collect and combine. I use these objects to create a language, tell a story, and build a world.

Although rusty and sometimes stuck, my recent body of work is about movement and seeing the humor in our circumstances. Each piece wants to get ahead and move faster — yet many drag a weight behind them, some have a shell to break through, and still others await takeoff. Through my work, I want to communicate the power of transformation as well as question standardized ideas about value. That could be why I am drawn to old and worn objects and spaces. I want to uncover their beauty, and give them a purpose — a new life filled with meaning. I somehow believe that if old things can be joined and transformed, then so can we.

Fiddlefoot. Mixed media construction, 10" x 19" x 3.5", 2010.

Ungrounded. Mixed media construction, 12" x 17.5" x 11", 2008.

Beatit. Mixed media construction,
13" x 7.5" x 3", 2008.

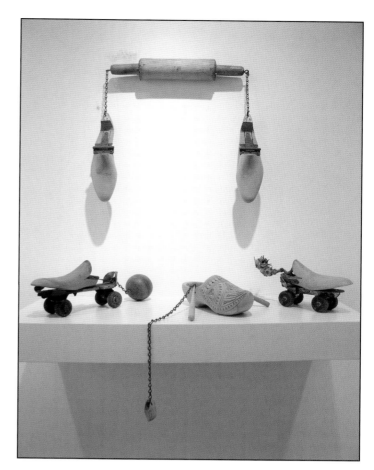

Feats. Installation, 36" x 48", 2009.

Clogged. Mixed media construction,
8" x 12" x 2.5", 2009.

Janet Orselli at OK Harris. Installation,
19'6" x 28" x 10-1/2", 2007.

Penny Overcash

Art mirrors life, intentionally or not. Age simplifies impulse. Importance and focus change as experience forces our hand. Connection and solitude form a balance just as fantasy and reality provide conviction and connotation. There is a need to create that overrides other occupations and opportunities. I embrace challenge and diversity, breaking a few rules along the way to feed my individual indulgence.

My recent work is inspired by past and present experience yet falls heavily on the fantasy side of expression. Life-changing events have led me to search for a balance between the intense and the whimsical nuances of human emotion and association. Fantasy and mystery have always been an attraction for me in all visual forms of artistic expression. The psychology of human emotion and reaction that can vary dramatically from one person to another is a constant theme for exploration. I am fascinated by patterns and forms in the organic sense and the patterns and paths we use to communicate that connect us all. I try to convey both dormancy and exposure in my work as I see it becoming a strong flux in this age of high technology, where we are hidden and yet are exposing so much of ourselves to so many.

The reaction to my sculpture seems to imply a personal journey for each viewer. I am always intrigued by what people see and feel when they connect with one of my pieces. A personal narrative becomes present, and the perception is unique for each person.

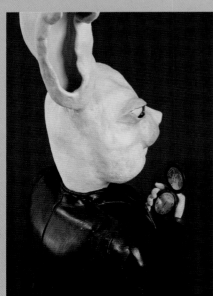

Late for Tea. Ceramic, wood, steel, acrylic paint, 37" x 15" x 10", 2011. *Courtesy of Mitchell Kearney.*

Emergence – A Narrative Connection. Ceramic, glazes. 12" x 21" x 12", 2011. Courtesy of Mitchell Kearney.

Alice – When She Was So Tall. Ceramic, oxide washes, glazes, and steel, 16" x 6", 2010. Courtesy of Mitchell Kearney.

Sideways. Ceramic, glazes, copper wire, steel glass beads, 19" x 9", 2010. Courtesy of Mitchell Kearney.

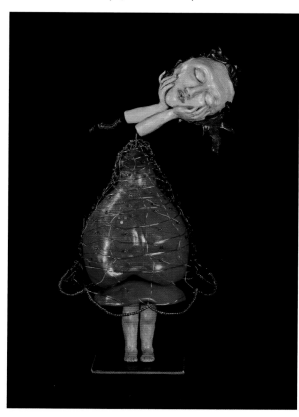

The Red Queen. Ceramic, glazes, glass beads, steel, polymer clay, 18" x 10", 2011. Courtesy of Mitchell Kearney.

Myrna Reiss

Moving to North Carolina was like opening a whole new chapter in my life… I had no idea that my path would take such a different direction. Just a few years ago, I quit my job as an executive and ran from the corporate world feeling drained, burned out, and beaten. I moved to Mooresville, a place with a wonderful old downtown, where no building is over two stories high. While exploring this little gem, I happened on a clock repair/pottery studio. My life truly changed when I walked in the door. The warmth, the welcome, the openness just grabbed me, and I decided to take lessons. Hanging out at the studio was like being a kid again hanging with my friends. We'd throw pots, laugh, and maybe have a glass of wine or two. After a few years, I found that the limited hours I spent at the shop just weren't enough. I was addicted to pottery and decided I had to have my own studio.

Throwing pottery is the closest I've ever come to meditation. The feel of the clay, watching it take shape, having my hands create a form from mud is so rewarding. Then there's playing with glazes to get just the look I want. Which is more organic? Opening the kiln is always exciting. Have I captured the look I wanted or have I serendipitously created something even better? Each part of the process absorbs me and brings me closer to what is real and makes me more a part of the South that I love.

I traded living the life of a nomadic corporate executive, following the almighty dollar for the life of a potter in Mooresville, North Carolina, and I couldn't be happier.

Courtesy of Patrick Tinkley Photography.

Crimson with blue flash. *Courtesy of Patrick Tinkley Photography.*

12" frozen lava red bowl. *Courtesy of Barbara Purchia.*

12" ghosted grey blue bowl. *Courtesy of Patrick Tinkley Photography.*

10" open red bowl.

Waiting for spring stemmie. *Courtesy of Patrick Tinkley Photography.*

Mary Ann Scherr

In the world of massive information and creative exchange, I have an ongoing, personal need to explore ideas, to alter directions, investigate new materials, and to review traditional processes.

Within this quest, there exists the desire to consciously intuit those elements which provide the focus to be open, receptive, and especially, to remain aware of the possibility of a discovery.

Courtesy of Penland School of Crafts/ David Ramsey, photographer.

Necklace-1. Japanese Netsuke. 14K gold, diamonds, sterling silver. Courtesy of Seth Tice-Lewis.

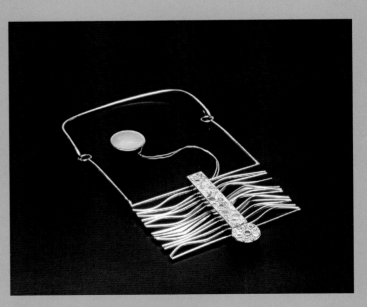

Body Monitor. 14K gold, sterling silver, electronics, fiber optics. *Courtesy of Seth Tice-Lewis.*

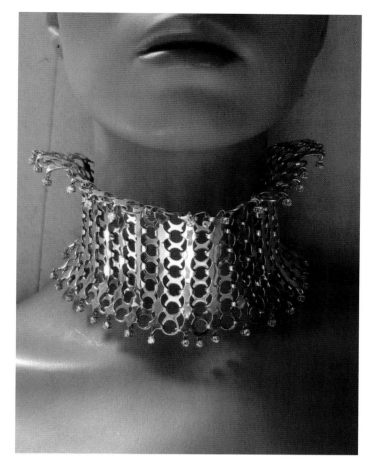

Neck-lace. 50 diamonds, 14K gold.

Waterfall necklace. Sterling silver. *Courtesy of Seth Tice-Lewis.*

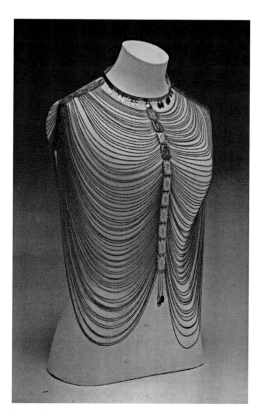

Dinka. Torso Necklace. 14K gold, sterling silver, emeralds. *Courtesy of David Ramsey.*

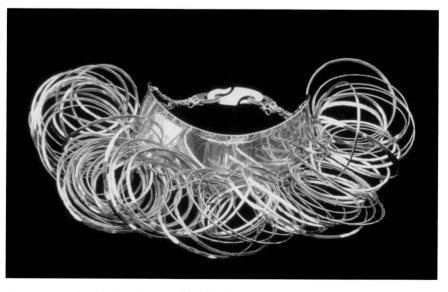

Loops necklace. Sterling silver. *Courtesy of Seth Tice-Lewis.*

Ebeth Scott-Sinclair

As a native Southerner, I am one of many generations who have called the Southeast United States home. I grew up surrounded by diverse layers of culture, spirituality, history, and humor, which reflected in a world of juxtaposition conjured on my canvases. I am always searching for the emotions, personalities, and stories of people, objects, and places. Use of texture and vibrant color help me create and then access the private, quiet voice of truth that is often hidden behind public facades. I have been asked if I see the world the way I paint it. Yes, I do. I simply translate the everyday into other possibilities.

Courtesy of Jessie Gladin-Kramer.

Sunflowers on Blue Checks. Acrylic, 12" x 12".

Home. Acrylic, 24" x 30".

Grandma's Bounty. Acrylic, 14" x 18".

Plenty. Acrylic, 12" x 12".

Sisters on the Porch. Acrylic, 36" x 24".

Leaving the Field. Acrylic, 36" x 12".

Pringle Teetor

Art has always been a part of my essential being. I began with clay, toddling behind my mother in Newcomb College's ceramics studio, where she would plop me down at an old kick wheel. The joy of creating something out of spinning clay is my earliest memory as an artist. Later, in grade school penmanship classes, I'd fill my paper with elaborate designs until finally removing the ink cartridge and painting with it.

Inspiration comes from life. Flying over our country's amazing landscape, I see the lines, colors, and patterns change or the blending colors in the evening sky. I try to reflect this in my art.

I call myself an "accidental glass blower." Setting up my business as a photographer, I tried glass on a whim. Feeling that molten glass on a pipe, the energy and constant motion, hooked me instantly! Its properties are at any time hot, cold, fluid, soft, brittle, or hard. This metamorphosis can take place instantly. You use your hand to form it, but you can't touch it. Opaque, transparent, shiny, or matte, in seconds of heat the piece on your pipe can be a work of art; then in the next second, it is a mess worthy only of the scrap bucket. There is no going back. It can be physically challenging and exhausting, a silently choreographed dance of heat and motion.

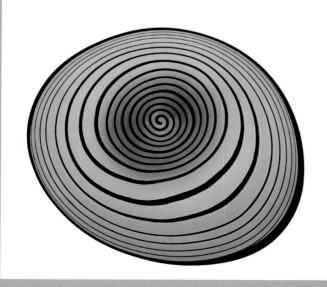

Pop art chartreuse wall piece, 5" x 18".

Black and white feathered vase, 10" x 7".

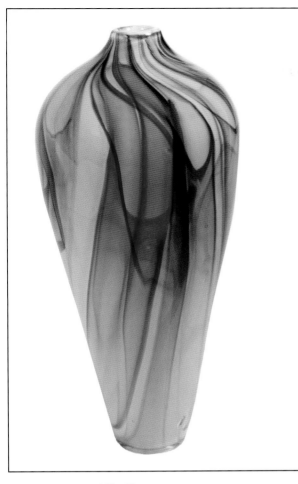

Color Field painting, 12" x 7".

Peacock feather vase, 10" x 7".

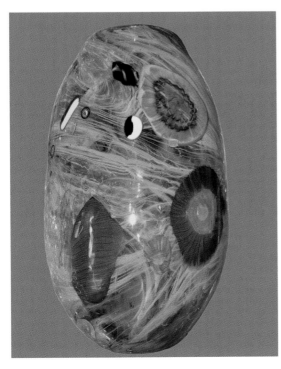

Seychelles island vase, 14" x 8".

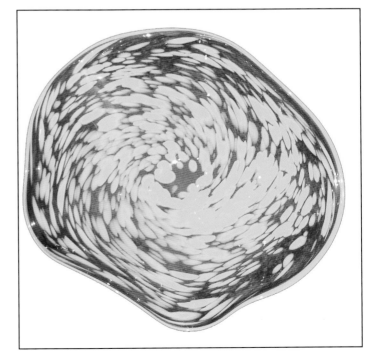

Canary yellow and red bowl, 8" x 15".

5.
South Carolina

Alice R. Ballard

My art is a reflection of my relationship with natural forms. These forms come to me on walks, while I work in my garden, on visits to the produce section of the grocery store, or appear as gifts from friends who share my fascination with the beauty inherent in nature's abundant variety of forms. To be more specific, it is often the metamorphosis of nature's forms as they change from season to season that attracts me. The southern seasons are particularly conducive to my process as they transition and recycle from year to year, distinct yet connected, and draw me into the universal world in which differing life forms share similar qualities. I spend countless hours contemplating a particular form in order to feel its energy. It becomes a Zen-like connection not unlike a meditation. Next I will begin to draw the form, trying to capture the essence of what I have felt and observed. Then I begin to bring this form to life in clay. As an artist, I hope that those who choose to connect with my work can share some of the harmony and tranquility I feel through the creative process. Perhaps, at the very least, the viewer will give those small, often unnoticed forms in nature, a second glance.

Courtesy of David Wilder.

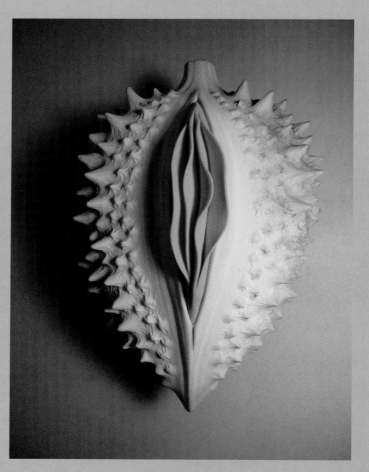

Pinch Pot. Red earthenware, terra sigillata, oxides, and liner glaze, 6" x 6" x 6", 2010.

Poppy Wall Pod. Red earthenware with terra sigillata and oxides, 11-1/2" x 10" x 6", 2010.

Pinch Pot. Earthenware with glaze liner, 6" x 6" x 6", 2010.

Pod Triangle II. Red and white earthenware, terra sigillata, and oxides, approx. 6" x 6" x 6", 2009.

Leaves, 28" x 6-8" x 3", 2010.

Long Pod Trio, 28" x 6" x 3-1/2", 2009.

Carl Blair

I have never looked at my paintings and sculptures as either realistic or abstract, even though they have elements of both, meaning they are abstracted representations of landscapes and animals, but also, at times, other subject matter. To me, the paintings are visual poetry and statements about nature and the aura that surrounds it, with an emphasis on the formal elements.

As poetic statements, the paintings inevitably are influenced by where I live or have lived. I was born Atchison, Kansas, in 1932, growing up as a farm boy. Many of my earlier work reflected that environment, suggesting flat landscapes with wide horizons and big skies. In 1957, I moved to Greenville, South Carolina. Today, we live on Paris Mountain, surrounded by forests, hills, rolling landscapes, and other vegetation; these are obvious elements in many of my paintings, even though they are imagined more than literal.

My sculptures also reflect my life and surroundings. They are of more-or-less imagined animals, created of wood and then painted. They have, I like to think, an expressive and whimsical, humorous quality. To some extent, I regard these creatures as self-portraits.

Courtesy of Hampton III Gallery.

Don't You Weep. Acrylic on canvas, 20" x 24", 2007.
Courtesy of if ART Gallery.

Last Goodbye. Acrylic on canvas, 20" x 24", 2008.
Courtesy of if ART Gallery.

Help, I've Got Something Stuck in My Bad Eye, But My Leg Feels a Lot Better. Polychrome wood, 23" x 28" x 1", 2008. Courtesy of if ART Gallery.

Tied To His Mother's Apron Strings. Polychrome wood, 20" x 24" x 12", 2008. Courtesy of if ART Gallery.

At His Wits End. Polychrome wood, 31" x 31" x 26", 2008. Courtesy of if ART Gallery.

Patti Brady

I spent a solid forty years living in coastal California cities, almost thirty of that in San Francisco, a city of wide-open vistas and fresh ocean breezes. When I moved to South Carolina in 1999, the dramatic change in landscape affected me profoundly. In San Francisco, we had a few flies and maybe a spider or two, but in South Carolina the air and ground are filled with flying things that dive-bomb into your eyes, nose, or eyes; then there's the cacophony of bugs that buzz, beetles, chirping crickets, cicadas, tree frogs, one hundred species of spiders, a few thousand mosquitoes, and no-see-ums. Throw in the mildew, humidity, thunder, and ice storms! Spring brings an eruption of plants, weeds, and kudzu growing at incredible speeds. It's all slightly claustrophobic for a costal Californian. This mass of visual stimulus seemed to couple innate obsessiveness with pattern, decorative elements, repeat design, botanical drawings, and "never enough color." My working process is to throw everything but the kitchen sink at the paper or canvas, simply luxuriating in the materials. (I have worked for Golden Artist Colors for seventeen years as an educator in use and technique of acrylic.) Although I seem to be extremely loose, there are many years of calculated play to know these materials and have them appear spontaneous. I work until I have a surface that is beautiful and precious to me. Then begins the work of making it a painting, pulling it back from the chaos, endless editing and adding back until it visually works as a finished piece.

Courtesy of Eli Warren.

Willy Nilly. Mixed media on paper, 27" x 27", 2009.
Courtesy of Eli Warren.

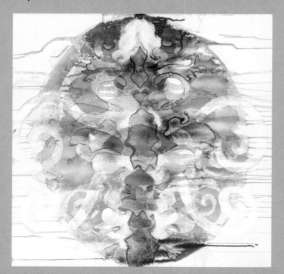

Awasharokoko. Mixed media on paper, 24" x 24", 2009.
Courtesy of Eli Warren.

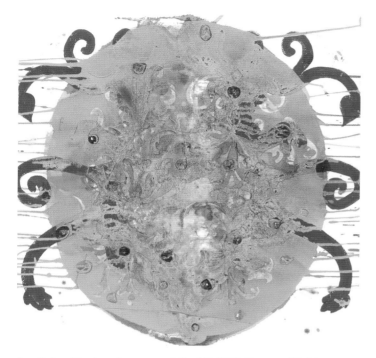

Aquatic Egg. Mixed media on paper, 24" x 24", 2009. *Courtesy of Eli Warren.*

Rosalee's Rose. Acrylic on plexi, 12" x 12", 2007. *Courtesy of Eli Warren.*

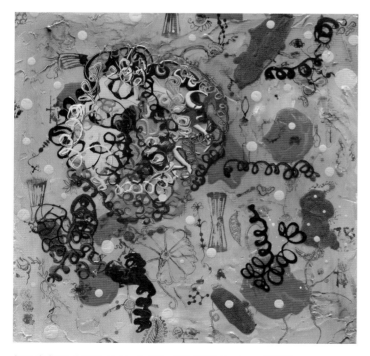

Loop de Loop. Acrylic on panel, 36" x 36", 2009. *Courtesy of Eli Warren.*

Blue Bonkers. Mixed media on paper, 27" x 27", 2009. *Courtesy of Eli Warren.*

Eva Carter

I call Charleston home because of the beauty of the Low Country. As the earthy aroma of pluff mud and the sounds of tidal activity waft into my studio from South Carolina's intercoastal waterway, I experience the passage of time through the ebb and flow of tides, the march of seasons, and cycles of new growth and decay.

The drama of weather conditions outside my Wadmalaw Island studio affects my brush stokes. As I approach the canvas, I feel the excitement of the weather changes from still low tides to rainstorms, from moon rises to color-drenched sunsets. Although I don't paint the literal landscape, my work emotionally responds to the outside world.

I work large scale. There's something about a big surface that really tests me, and I like the challenge. The large canvas pressures me to use my whole body and mind to paint. It's a very fulfilling and physical act. I have conviction in each decision I make on the canvas. While some of my strokes may be fast, other strokes take careful consideration. My paintings record that process of reaction and contemplation.

Courtesy of Karin Olah.

Extremes. Oil on canvas diptych, 90" x 144", 2003. *Courtesy of Rick Rhodes.*

In Plain Sight. Oil on canvas, 72" x 66", 2010. *Courtesy of Landis Powers.*

Amber Moment. Oil on canvas, 50" x 64", 2008. *Courtesy of Karin Olah.*

Spring Canopy. Oil on canvas, 60" x 66", 2008. *Courtesy of Karin Olah.*

Intention. Oil on canvas, 72" x 66", 2010. *Courtesy of Landis Powers.*

Jeff Donovan

I have two methods of generating images for paintings, one linear and one tonal. The linear method is more commonly known as "doodling" and has the spontaneous character of automatic writing and free association. The tonal method is less spontaneous and involves covering a surface with an uneven wash of a single color and then staring at it until the variations in value begin to suggest forms and volumes in space, which are then defined and developed further. As the resulting forms are almost always figurative, it is appropriate to say that the compositions are "fleshed out."

Both methods rely heavily on intuition and the subconscious, so I rarely know what a piece is about. Nor do I know its source in my experience, until I've had time to ponder it. That makes it difficult to say exactly what affect southern culture has had on my work, though in recent years certain subjects have come up that owe an obvious debt to the region. Pieces like Fat Back, Skeeter, and Southern Mansion are cases in point. I might speculate further that my preference for rich, multi-layered color and distressed, stained surfaces may, in large part, be due to my thirty-four-year residency in the South.

Courtesy of Ashleigh Burke Coleman.

Twist & Shout. Pastel and gouache on canvas, 24" x 24", 2010. *Courtesy of Ashleigh Burke Coleman.*

Embrace. Acrylic, gouache, charcoal, pastel on canvas, 19-1/2" x 21", 2010.
Courtesy of Ashleigh Burke Coleman.

OMAGAWD. Oil on canvas, 23" x 23", 2010.
Courtesy of Ashleigh Burke Coleman.

Southern Mansion. Ceramic, 14-1/2" x 7" x 10", 2010.
Courtesy of Ashleigh Burke Coleman.

Skeeter. Gouache, charcoal, pastel on canvas, 16" x 18", 2010.
Courtesy of Ashleigh Burke Coleman.

Toni Elkins

I absolutely adore being born and raised in the South! The people are so friendly, and bringing a pie to someone's door when they first move into town is not unusual. In fact, "warm and fuzzy" could describe most of my friends. The South has been good to me. I was born in Tifton, Georgia, but I have lived my adult life in Columbia, South Carolina.

Being from South Carolina is much like being from the other southern states. Columbia is a capital city, but it still has a small town atmosphere. My art reflects my personal experiences and serves as therapy for my soul. Being surrounded by my southern peers has added new dimensions to my art. I paint abstractly, but I define realistically in my mind. I do not plan ahead of time. I live in the moment and paint strictly from inner emotions. As in most artists' careers, I painted realism from the start. I began to come to the conclusion that seeing with a realistic eye and painting abstractly fit my personality. Those solid white canvases are intimidating! I like to see my work with fresh eyes — like entering a text from a new direction each time. I am never bored, and my art revives my spirit with new energy every day.

Alone. Acrylic on canvas, 28" x 38", 2010.

Peace. Acrylic on paper, 22" x 15", 2009.

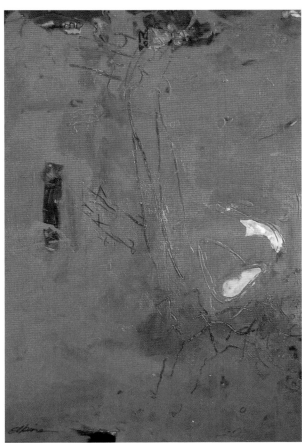

Peace and War. Acrylic on paper, 22" x 15.5", 2009.

Long Road Home. Acrylic on board, 35.5" x 25.5", 2009.

Phil Garrett

I spent my early years in the Piedmont of South Carolina and my 20s and early 30s in Hawaii and Northern California, where I studied art. In 1979, I returned to a South Carolina that felt more hospitable to artists than when I left and a place rich in contradictions. This contrariness is for some reason the proverbial grit that irritates, layers, and ultimately drives me. All the art I've seen and heard and felt in my life has shaped my visual aesthetic.

It is nature, in the end, a kind of mythical nature that informs my work: the power of storms; the spiritual quality of the elements; the beauty, grace, and ferocity of plants and animals — something beyond myself, something beyond an easy comprehension. Painting and making works on paper focuses my search for the mystery within the subject and within myself.

Courtesy of Eli Corbin.

Kyoto Variation - Lotus VIII. Monotype with chine colle, 32" x 25", 2007.

Thistle II (Hunting Island). Monotype with chine colle, 30" x 20", 2003. *Courtesy of Eli Warren.*

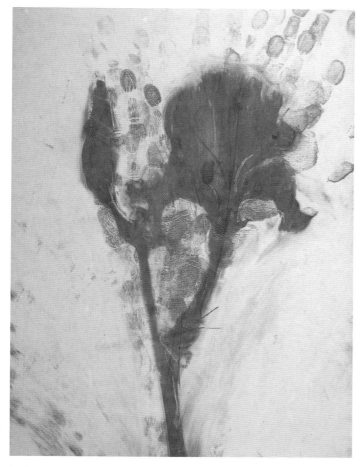

Kyoto Variation (Eupatorium) I. Monotype with chine colle, 35" x 30", 2006. *Courtesy of Eli Warren.*

Iris Strata I. Monotype with chine colle, 30" x 22", 2005.

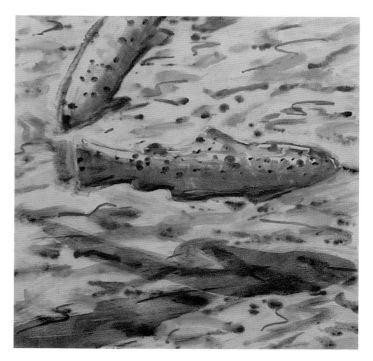

Penland Trout II. Acrylic painting on panel, 24" x 20", 2011.

Penland Trout Variation IV. Monotype with chine colle, 30" x 22", 2010.

Mana Hewitt

I was born into a military family traveling the United States and Europe until finally landing in South Carolina some forty years ago. With a southern mother who was also an art teacher, I was drawn to art almost from infancy. Though I am not a natural born Southerner, my years here have given me a sense of place. The South with its conflicted history and rich traditions of storytelling has been a tremendous influence on my art and me. I am compelled to tell visual stories, to experiment with new processes, and to broach social and political ideas. This has led to an ever-expanding number of subjects and media that I employ. Most of my works explore some sort of word play through imagery associated with the figure, technology, and the environment. Composed of multiply layered etched copper, brass nickel, sterling, cast figures, and found objects, they set the stage for the viewer to interpret the tale. My goal is to create work that is aesthetically pleasing and conceptually interesting.

Courtesy of Steven Hewitt.

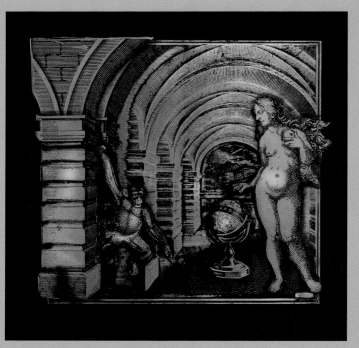

Intelligent Design: EVE. Etched copper on wood, 24" x 24" x 3", 2008.

Intelligent Design: 1, 2, 3, & 4. Etched copper on wood, 48" x 48" x 3", 2009.

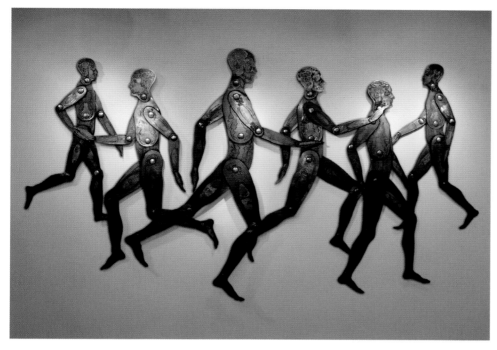

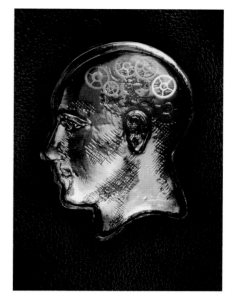

Financial Figures. Etched copper on wood, 10" x 6" x 4", 2006.

The Mechanics of Memory (Brooch). Etched sterling, brass, and resin, 3" x 2" x .25", 2010.

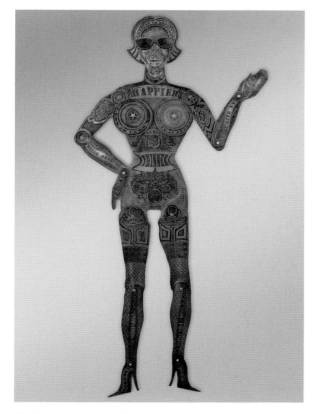

The Mechanics of Desire. Etched copper and brass, 42" x 32" x 3", 2005.

The Silenced Majority. Etched copper, brass, and nickel on wood, 42" x 32" x 3", 2006.

Peter Lenzo

The impetus for my ceramic sculptures came from traditional Southern face jugs. I had switched to working in clay exclusively in the 1990s. I had been making sculptural assemblages but had to stop because I couldn't use a table saw any longer as I increasingly suffered from seizures, which are the result of brain damage sustained in a bicycle accident in my youth. Table saws and seizures don't mix.

I always had been intrigued by face jugs, especially those made by southern slaves. At my middle school, we tried to develop teaching materials that appealed to our African-American students; so I decided to have them make face jugs. I had never made any, so I first created several. The first ones I didn't quite like, and so I made some more. Each batch got better, but more importantly, when I finished a batch, I couldn't wait to make the next one. It just seemed to be in my bones. It felt like I had made them before — that I was catching up where I had left off. I wanted to let everything go in my current life and go back to a previous one that I had discovered. I once was lost and now was found.

From the jugs, I came to the current, more elaborate sculptures. It started when my then four-year-old son Joe started to stick pottery chards, which I used for teeth, in one of my jugs. All over: nose, eyes, and lips. He went wild. Then he started to stick other objects in them, like a ceramic snake. I began to help him and gradually really liked the results. My style was very different, and I had much more respect for the face, but to this day, Joe claims that he made me famous.

Courtesy of if ART Gallery.

Life Or Death. Stoneware, nichrome wire, porcelain, glazes, slip, found objects, 19" x 16" x 9", 2009. *Courtesy of Jim Hulin, PeterLenzoPottery.com.*

Sicilian 3d Eye Shard. Stoneware, nichrome wire, porcelain, glazes, slip, found objects, 22" x 12" x 5", 2005. *Courtesy of Jim Hulin, PeterLenzoPottery.com.*

Countdown: Alligator Love. Stoneware, nichrome wire, porcelain, glazes, slip, found objects, 13.5" x 7" x 6", 2008. *Courtesy of Jim Hulin, PeterLenzoPottery.com.*

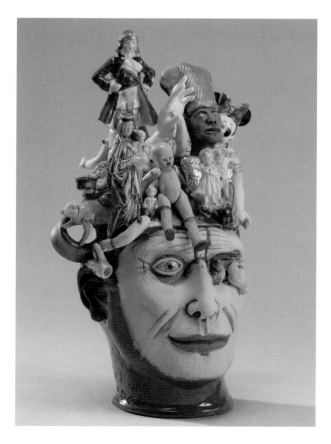

59 Countdown: Happy 18th Roxanne. Stoneware, nichrome wire, porcelain, glazes, slip, found objects, 13.5" x 8.5" x 6", 2008. *Courtesy of Jim Hulin, PeterLenzoPottery.com.*

Tjelda vander Meijden

My work explores the transient nature of our time on earth — an ever-changing place of refuge and peril — and the quest for immortality inherent in the human spirit. The acceleration of global climate change, particularly with respect to water, inspires the issues of transformation and impermanence in my art and compels me to grapple with the many complexities of this emerging reality.

In order to experience and paint the retreating glaciers and diminishing ice flows, I traveled to the harshest most isolated places on earth including Antarctic Peninsula, Ushuaia, High Arctic Islands, and Iceland. Living at the sea's edge gave me a very palpable sense of this elemental life force and the massive effort it will take for mankind to address the ever-present challenges of sustaining life on earth. It is my hope that the viewer will experience the power of this epic battle between man and nature as it is revealed, metaphorically, through my work.

Present Water, 2010. Monotype, 11" x 17". Courtesy of Rick Rhodes.

Disappearing Ice #324, 2010. Oil on canvas, 48" x 36". Courtesy of Rick Rhodes.

Forced Migration, 2010. Monotype, 16" x 20". Courtesy of Rick Rhodes.

Life at the Edge, 2010. Monotype, 11" x 17". Courtesy of Rick Rhodes.

Seemingly Irreversible, 2008. Oil on canvas, 48" x 36".
Courtesy of Rick Rhodes.

Profound Silence, 2007. Oil on canvas, 48" x 36". Courtesy of Rick Rhodes.

Dorothy Netherland

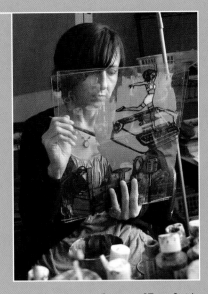

Courtesy of Tyson Smith.

Making drawings from pictures I find in vintage women's magazines helps me explore my ideas about family and identity, the distortion of memory, and transience. Working in reverse on two or three panes of glass which will later be stacked together, I make multiple overlapping drawings with ink and acrylic paint, continuously scraping away and re-applying new imagery and color. My work has evolved to include imagery that is scraped, painted, screen printed, ink transferred from my past paintings, and etched onto the surface of the glass.

The predominantly figurative imagery in my work is not arrived at through a sense of nostalgia, and I don't feel as though I'm making cultural observations, or contrasting the comparative innocence of a past time with today's ironic self-awareness. The people who populate my paintings are transformed from their original context as product sellers into my cast of characters, who now seem to be conveying ideas about self-hood. I am responding to the idea of the past as something that is interpreted, rather than remembered. I am interested in the ways in which we frame our own personal narratives and the power of the imagination to fill in the blanks. I find it fascinating that our current identities are culled from such vague recollections. Underneath a slick surface, I suggest associations that may be false or intangible, like fragments of memory. Living in Charleston, a place endowed with such a rich and conflicting history, makes the South seem like the best place to make art informed by these ideas.

Look At Me. Ink, acrylic, screen print, ink transfer, and glass etching on glass, 16" x 20", 2011. *Courtesy of Nancy Santos.*

Devotion. Ink, acrylic, screen print, ink transfer, and glass etching on glass, 16" x 20", 2011. *Courtesy of Nancy Santos.*

When You Were a Little Girl 1. Ink, acrylic, and screen print on glass, 16" x 16", 2009. *Courtesy of Townsend Davidson.*

When You Were a Little Girl 2. Ink, acrylic, and screen print on glass, 16" x 16", 2009. *Courtesy of Townsend Davidson.*

Matt Overend

My work is best described as originating in solitude. Essentially, the subject of my painting, whether still life, landscape or architectural study, is personal isolation, solitude, and a sense of quiet solitude. As what an artist paints becomes what he sees and what he sees eventually becomes what he feels, so my paintings are influenced by being here in South Carolina. In particular, the landscapes, the road and field studies, and the pine trees, are, of course, determined in every actual sense, by the air, the light, and, above all, by how the sky meets the horizon. That flat straight-arrow edge of earth, when placed in relation to the vertical and horizontal edges of the canvas, creates immediate design with an architectural quality. This design provides an opportunity for variation and encourages a search for composition that is balanced but not necessarily symmetrical. This balance is achieved through unique compositional arrangements that use the center of the canvas as the point of departure. The flat horizon, the black shadow pines, the roads with their white and yellow painted lines, the occasional stop sign, are what I see, what I paint, and now what I feel.

Many of the formal elements of my landscape paintings also work their way into my other work, but some of those also go back to the non-representational, even hard-edge work I did in the 1980s. I used the straight edge and a T-square instead of free-handing it. That came out of my training as an engineer. It seemed as natural to me as using a brush.

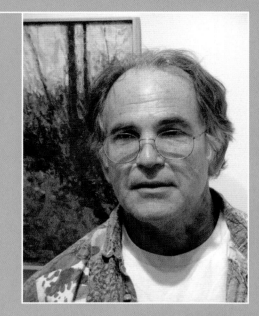

Courtesy of if ART Gallery.

Architectural Study No.2. Oil on canvas, 20" x 18", 2011.
Courtesy of if ART Gallery.

Architectural Study No. 4. Oil on canvas, 24" x 28", 2011.
Courtesy if ART Gallery.

Road Study No. 318. Oil on canvas, 20" x 12", 2008.
Courtesy of Ashleigh Burke Coleman.

Road Study No. 322. Oil on canvas, 17" x 14", 2008.
Courtesy of Ashleigh Burke Coleman.

Summer Field. Oil on canvas, 24" x 19", 2009.
Courtesy of Ashleigh Burke Coleman.

Edward Rice

My studio is located in my hometown of North Augusta, South Carolina. My mother's ancestors arrived in this area in the mid-eighteenth century; my father's forbearers arrived here in the mid-nineteenth century. My studio, originally built as the town jail, was converted to a cottage by my grandfather. I acquired the building in 1990 and renovated it to use as a studio. I raised the roof and put in skylights, central air, and heat. Where I paint today is the same room I used to draw and paint in as a child. My main worktable stands right where my grandmother's dining table sat. I spent many hours at that table so long ago. Obviously, I have a long history with the place. Although I travel quite a lot in the Unites States and beyond, this is the place I am always anxious to get back to. This is evident in my work.

Courtesy of John Harpring.

Dormer, Noon. Oil on canvas, 48" x 48", 2010.
Courtesy of John Harpring.

Gable, Botany Bay. Oil on canvas, 48" x 36", 2010.
Courtesy of John Harpring.

Charleston Cupola. Oil on canvas, 48" x 30", 2011.
Courtesy of John Harpring.

Meadow Garden. Oil on canvas, 30" x 24", 2008-10.
Courtesy of John Harpring.

Carpenter Gothic. Oil on canvas, 60" x 42", 2009-10.
Courtesy of John Harpring.

Dormer with Mansard Roof. Oil on canvas, 60" x 42", 2010.
Courtesy of John Harpring.

Virginia Scotchie

The idea of taking from one object and connecting it to another through the dissection of parts and pieces is a foundation of my recent work in ceramic sculpture. Combined with this is my interest in the relation of whole forms to that of fragments. Exploration in the studio is an on-going visual investigation of man-made and natural objects. Usually these consist of small things ordinary in many ways, but possessing an odd quirkiness that pulls me to them. A recent object, for example, was a handmade wooden tool that was fashioned by my Italian grandfather to plant his garden. For me, it not only holds visual intrigue but also a connection to my memory of him and the things he loved.

In the past five years, I have continued my investigation of ceramic sculpture with a desire and drive to push into new territories of creative research. My work has been exhibited across the country in both invitational and group exhibitions. Internationally, I have shown in France, Australia, Italy, Taiwan, and China in the past five years. I have recently begun work on a collaborative project, which was partially supported by the Department of Art and the USC Arts Institute called the Crucible Project. Five internationally recognized artists and myself work together once a semester to create new work that focuses on the crucible as a premise. This work will begin a national tour in 2012 starting at the Columbia Museum of Art.

Around the World (front and side views). Stoneware, glazed in multiple firings, 84" x 12" x 84", 2010. *Courtesy of David Ramsey.*

Salmon Spout Bowl. Stoneware, glazed in multiple firings, 13" x 22" x 22", 2008. *Courtesy of David Ramsey.*

Turquoise Knob Spout (wall piece). Glazed in multiple firings, 30" x 15" x 20", 2009. *Courtesy of David Ramsey.*

Two views of *Slate Bronze House Bowl.* Stoneware, glazed in multiple firings, 13" x 12" x 21", 2010. *Courtesy of David Ramsey.*

Laura Spong

Although I am a painter in the South, where I have lived all my life, I don't see myself as a "southern artist." I am an abstract expressionist, and as such it's hard to define a direct connection between my region and the content and aesthetics of my work. That's not to say no connection exists. My paintings are in the final analysis about me, and I am influenced by my surroundings and the people in it.

First of all, I like to paint — it's my passion. I move shapes, forms, textures, and colors until the components fall into place, like a child on the floor arranging and rearranging blocks. My goal is to portray, visually, in a non-objective manner, my own inner journey as I search for meaning and purpose in life. I hope to make a connection with others on a similar journey. I believe that everything is connected, a part of the whole.

Within this context, the way my paintings turn out, including their mood, is influenced by what goes on in my life. Interacting with people, seeing other artists' work, reading books and articles, taking in the news, experiencing what goes on around me — all that influences my state of mind, which has an impact on my paintings. Living in the South obviously is a factor in all this.

The South most likely also contributed to my late start as an artist. Few women of my generation around here took this path, and as a mother of six in a conventional marriage, my earlier years provided few opportunities to develop as an artist. Living in the South also facilitated my considerable lack of awareness of what went on in the arts nationally and internationally, which helped me set my own, independent course.

Courtesy of if ART Gallery.

Restored. Oil on canvas, 36" x 36", 2010.
Courtesy of Ashleigh Burke Coleman.

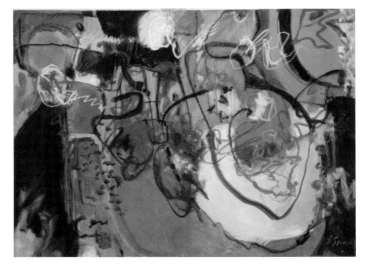

Dancing To An Unnamed Tune. Oil on canvas, 36" x 48", 2011. *Courtesy of if ART Gallery.*

A Discreet Happening. Oil on canvas, 30" x 30", 2011. *Courtesy of if ART Gallery.*

Sunless Riddle. Oil on canvas, 36" x 36", 2010. *Courtesy of Ashleigh Burke Coleman.*

Once In A Green Moon. Oil on canvas, 40" x 90" (triptych, 40" x 30" ea.), 2010. *Courtesy of Ashleigh Burke Coleman.*

Leo Twiggs

Every artist must create out of his own being, out of the result of his own encounter with the world. I was born in the South and, needless to say, the things I remember, the scents, the atmosphere, all acted to shape the imagery I use in my paintings.

Very often people ask me how I came to work in the medium of batik, why I picked this ancient medium rather than more contemporary techniques. Some have even written that it is my African ancestry that drew me to the medium because batiks have been used in Africa to decorate textiles, but a medium is merely a tool for the artist to help him achieve his magic. All I know is that I wanted to get a specific feeling in my work, and batik allowed me to get it.

We were poor folks, and I remember a pervasive kind of dinginess, a kind of "oldness," of not having the new, but there was always a dignity in it all. Somewhere along the way, I saw the spidery web-like linear patterns and mottled surface inherent to batik as expressive of an aging process, the struggle to survive, not just the world, but time itself. I came to realize that the struggle we had was the basic struggle of mankind — we were not alone. Perhaps that is why my figures evolved to be no longer just black or brown, but purple (lots of purple, even now I don't know why), red, blue, yellow, and white.

Thoreau once said that the mass of mankind live out lives of quiet desperation. Perhaps it is the quiet but universal desperation I sought to portray in my work.

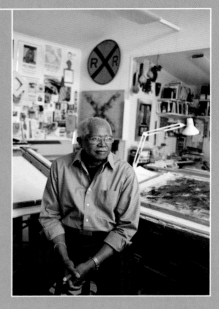

Courtesy of Jerry Siegel.

Anchored In the Spirit. Batik on cotton, 26" x 23", 2001.

Milestones 1 (Flag Series). Batik on cotton, 29" x 37", 2010.

Seeking Sanctuary #3. Batik on cotton, 25" x 24-1/2", 2005.

Targeted Man #2. Batik on cotton, 26-1/2" x 26-1/2", 2007.

We Have Known Rivers: Ancestors Watching. Batik on cotton, 41" x 28", 1992.

County Fair. Batik on cotton, 19" x 24", 2008.

Mary Walker

I live and work in beautiful isolation on Johns Island, South Carolina, where I moved to as a newlywed from New York in 1975. Surrounded by marsh and water, the colors in fall, winter, and spring turn to earthy browns and ochres with the silvery sky reflected in the water. This light, these colors influence my palette.

As a narrative artist, I am fascinated by people — our virtues, sorrows, and foibles. Using the figure, literally and as a metaphor, my goal is to inject human comedy and tragedy into my work. Literature, particularly Shakespeare, Dante, and southern writers including Faulkner and Flannery O'Connor, is a source of inspiration. The symbolism and meaning in The Stations of the Cross, the human frailties of Pinocchio, the drama and revenge in the Orestian Trilogy all are wellsprings for my art. I aim to express the rich tapestry of life, weaving the elements of the human condition into the work. My goal is to reduce the imagery to its essential symbolic expression.

Courtesy of Lese Corrigan.

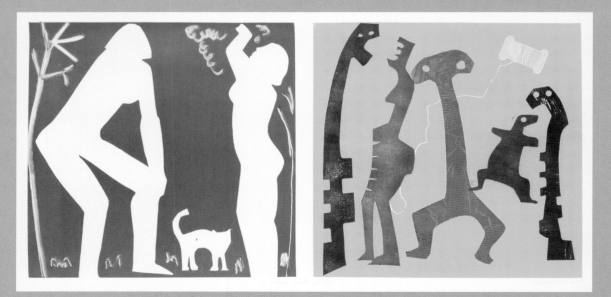

Blue and Yellows. Monotype, 14" x 29", 2010. *Courtesy of Rick Rhodes.*

Here Birdie. Monotype, 14" x 14", 2010. *Courtesy of Rick Rhodes.*

Lady Godiva. Oil on canvas, 24" x 24", 2010. *Courtesy of James Zimmeran.*

Cat in Window. Oil on board, 16" x 11", 2009. *Courtesy of James Zimmeran.*

Guess Who I Saw Today. Oil on panel, 36" x 24", 2005.
Courtesy of Lese Corrigan.

Enid Williams

My work addresses the nature of pictorial perception as it relates to the broader topic of abstraction. Working in the South has been a productive chapter in my career, introducing me to an entirely new artistic community. My work has benefited from this expanded dialogue, resulting in new exhibition opportunities and opportunities for collaborative projects. Regardless of context, I have found engaged audiences in the region, responsive to the optical complexity that characterizes my work and intrigued to discover that color perception charts served as my initial inspiration. My vocabulary of circular shapes reveals a commitment to gestural mark making and classical ideals of beauty.

Pleasure Zone. Oil on canvas, 60" x 60", 2010.
Courtesy of Eli Warren Photography.

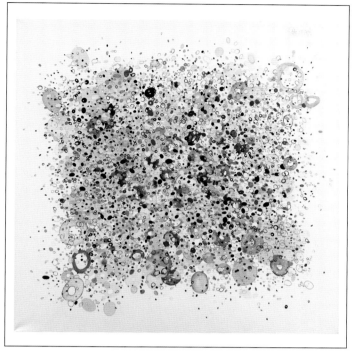

Remix. Enamel on canvas, 48" x 48", 2009.
Courtesy of Eli Warren Photography.

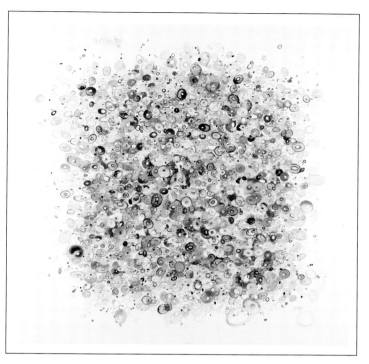

Late Bloomer. Oil on canvas, 60" x 60", 2010.
Courtesy of Eli Warren Photography.

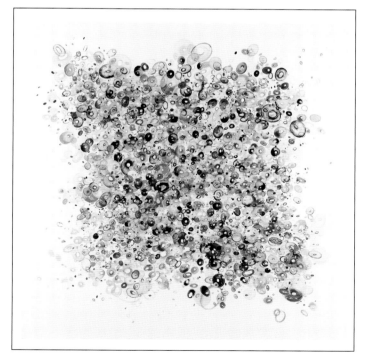

Modern Organic. Oil on canvas, 60" x 60", 2010.
Courtesy of Eli Warren Photography.

Shortwave Scatter. Oil on canvas, 60" x 60", 2010.
Courtesy of Eli Warren Photography.

Mike Williams

Comfortable year-round weather and an abundance of flora and fauna make South Carolina a natural paradise. With the lower end of the Appalachian Trail in the upstate, the Atlantic coastline to the East, and the Savannah River forming our border to the West, we have a diverse range of geographical topography.

Of particular interest to me is the flooded timber and wetland terrain, which offers an ambiguous relationship between wood, water, and air, creating a spatially complex and intriguing visual feast. I have been transfixed by the natural world surrounding me for as long as I can remember, spending countless hours fishing, hunting, and observing nature in an area encompassing the Congaree, the Wateree, and the upper Santee rivers. In my younger years, I even contemplated living my life on a floating house hitched to a cypress tree along the Santee.

In 1988, however, I made a choice that allows me to record and preserve my experiences growing up in the South through the creation of art. One category of my paintings and the majority of my sculptures have fish as the primary subject in an ever-shifting symbolist manner. The second category of my paintings focuses on aquatic landscapes, with an emphasis on atmospheric conditions, time, and space. All of my artwork is derived from my experiences as an outdoorsman, my fascination with the creative process, and my interest in modern art. I view my work as a visual collective of the conscious mind, tempered by the unconscious and the music in my ears.

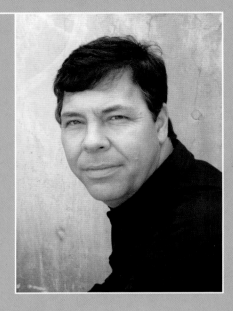

Suspending Forms XXV. Acrylic and ink on canvas, 60" x 60", ©2009.

Tide. Acrylic and ink on canvas, 36" x 36", ©2011.

Orientation, Number 2. Acrylic and ink on canvas, 20" x 34.5", ©2000.

First Five. Acrylic and ink on canvas, 48" x 60", 2011.

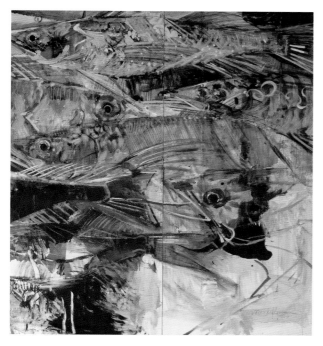

On the Verge IV. Acrylic and ink on panels (diptych), 80" x 72", ©2010.

This Way and That. Acrylic and ink on panels (triptych), 80" x 96", ©2011.

David H. Yaghjian

The South is quirky, intense, dark, and musky.
It is a land of poisonous serpents,
and voracious vines.
The heat and the humidity are primeval.
It feels biblical, mythic.
It terrified me. But then lots of things do.
I have lived here most of my life.
I am a Southerner by birth, but not by lineage.
My father came to the U.S. from Armenia.
My mother came from New Jersey.

If my last name weren't enough to set me apart, my temperament was. I stood on the sidelines and observed. I felt different and went inward. I saw, heard, and experienced with my eyes and imagination. In high school the idea of William Blake appealed to me; I spent lunches in the library reading Edward Albee plays.

Both my parents were painters; I got the genes. Earlier in my career, I sort of coasted on "talent." Growing up in a small city where my parents were relatively big fish, I assumed there would be a coronation, and I would take on my father's mantle. Didn't happen. In spite of the delusions and dissoluteness, I have had some successes. I sold work to a New York patron, who also commissioned half a dozen portraits. Got into good galleries in Atlanta and South Carolina. Got married, had a daughter. Grew up a bit.

After years of working apart from others, I got a studio in a space with twelve other artists. It was a revelation. I saw how other artists functioned. They struggled, did laundry, had kids to take care of, cars that broke down, sometimes they had money, sometimes they didn't. Being in this community allowed me to become more realistic about work and life schedules and to hit a stride that feels sustainable.

Bird. Oil, 14" x 11", 2007.

Man with Dog in Hand. Painted wood, 15" x 18" x 8", 2011.

Three Trout. Oil, 30" x 30", 2007.

Scene VI. Oil, 12" x 16", 2011.

Weight Lifter. Painted wood, 26" x 26" x 12", 2011.

Paul Yanko

The artistic community based in South Carolina is comprised of a diverse and prolific set of members. I have benefitted professionally from having an opportunity to both contribute and receive insights from painters, sculptors, and others working in an extensive range of disciplines. Artists of this region represent both long- and short-term residency in the South. Educational influences of these individuals are equally diverse, ranging from training and apprenticeship in the region to extensive research abroad.

Since locating to the upstate of South Carolina, I have become increasingly focused on developing a response to abstraction that addresses nuances of color and surface and the combination of flat and illusionistic space. I develop my paintings systematically over periods of time that can extend from several months to three or more years. The surfaces of my work acquire a relief-like quality as I apply acrylic paint mixed with various mediums over masked areas. My palette is extensively based on the use of saturated hues organized in contrasting color schemes. As configurations of densely clustered shapes emerge, I continue to embellish successively smaller shapes over larger underlying rectilinear and geometric shapes.

Artist with his painting, *Pleasure Zone*, in the background.

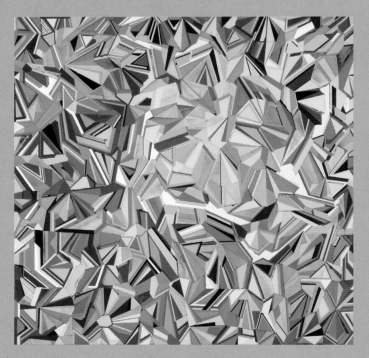

Green Wing Grid. Acrylic on canvas, 30" x 30", 2008-09. *Courtesy of Eli Warren.*

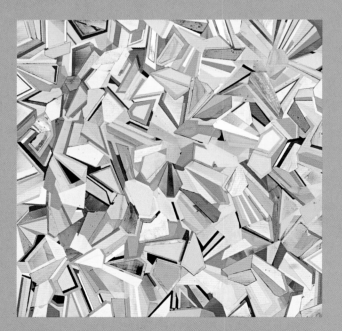

Hub Angle Ray. Acrylic on canvas, 20" x 20", 2007. *Courtesy of Eli Warren.*

Box Module Angle. Mixed media on panel, 12-1/4" x 12-1/4", 2010.
Courtesy of Eli Warren.

Cluster Wing Tilt. Acrylic on canvas, 50" x 42", 2009-10.
Courtesy of Eli Warren.

Red Fan Gate. Acrylic on canvas, 48" x 36", 2007.
Courtesy of Eli Warren.

Module Bloom Slant. Acrylic on canvas, 14" x 14", 2008-09.
Courtesy of Eli Warren.

Linda S. Young

Being in the South brings a different way of life that is certainly calmer and gentler than before. I am transformed into another world when walking on the beach just looking for sharks' teeth or interesting shells. No rush, no deadlines, just being. There, ideas can flow freely in my mind, and some of my best paintings come from those inspirations.

As I work, a spirit envelopes me and I am in another world. I paint intuitively, choosing colors that my mind sees to show what I am feeling inside. Each stroke is put down sometimes without thinking, and I try not to let the intellect interfere with that spark of creativity. I get excited when the painting has a spirit of its own.

At times those strokes or colors are not quite right but adding them anyway brings me to the next step. Every now and then, I wonder how that color or stroke got there; sometimes I question why I didn't put this or that in the painting, but I know that the painting was done from that spirit inside me. Through my years of being an artist, I am able to see what needs to be tweaked. The beauty of this area permeates everything I do, and I am privileged to be able to live here and paint its incredible splendor.

Courtesy of Jane Staszak.

Carrie Ready to Fledge. Pastel, 15" x 17", 2011.

A Walk in the Dunes. Pastel, 34" x 29", 2011.

Autumn. Pastel, 16" x 16", 2010.

Sunset. Pastel, 16" x 16", 2010.

Calm. Pastel, 12" x 16", 2010.

Don Zurlo

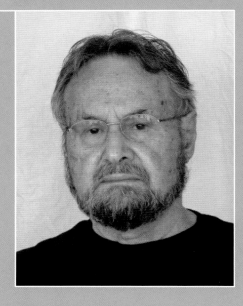

While living in South Carolina, I have become more conscious of the focus in my work on an altered sense of reality, a reflection of the uncertainty and anxiety of the contemporary world. Our perceptions of reality are arbitrary, in a constant state of flux. My own understanding is subjective and continually evolving.

Ambiguities of life in the South, in particular, exist in a culture of extreme attitudes and perceptions based on inherited experiences from a society centuries in the past in conflict with the changing realities of modern life. I suffer from my own internal conflicts, born in the Northeast but having lived in the South since 1973. My life and works are continually changing and in various stages of conflict — tearing and reassembling a collage of overlapping layers of contradictory impulses, ideas, and experiences. My impulses often direct my painting toward a spontaneous, physical expression of the energy and optimism of youth, an escape from the tortured and often erroneous rational processes of this world. The challenge continues as it has the last fifty years — an almost Zen-like task — to create order out of the constant chaos in my life and my world. In a universal sense, I create an art style that reflects the arbitrary nature of existence existing in harmonious balance with the universe.

New Mexico 271. Acrylic on canvas, 60" x 48", 2006.

Sante Fe 2. Acrylic on canvas, 48" x 48", 2006.

Sante Fe 3. Acrylic on canvas, 48" x 60", 2006.

New Mexico 53. Acrylic on canvas, 48" x 60", 2006.

Blooming Bush. Acrylic on canvas, 30" x 40", 2007.

Jeanne Goodman

I was born and raised in the metropolitan New York City area but have lived for the past thirty years in southeastern Virginia. Since moving to Norfolk, Virginia, I have witnessed the establishment and growth of an orthodox Jewish community in my neighborhood, similar to what I remember in New Rochelle, New York. As I became more aware of the emergence of this Hasidic community around me, I began to develop this series of drawings about Hasidim.

As an artist, my colored pencil drawings are often figurative images, people and animals alike. I primarily draw with colored pencils and colored pencil art sticks. I try to incorporate the stray lines and under-drawings to enhance a sense of movement and immediacy that is so important an element in my work. With these drawings, the shapes in the groups of Hasidim challenge me both artistically and intellectually. I feel strongly that my technique is effective as I portray the raw texture of the orthodox Jewish lifestyle and the energy of the group process they create.

Courtesy of Mark Robbins Photography.

The Minyan. Colored pencil on Rives BFK, 40" x 30", 2010. *Courtesy of Mark Robbins Photography.*

In Discussion. Colored pencil on Rives BFK, 22" x 28", 2010.
Courtesy of Mark Robbins Photography.

Dancing the Hora. Colored pencil on Rives BFK, 24" x 36", 2010.
Courtesy of Mark Robbins Photography.

Cow on Left. Colored pencil on Rives BFK, 14" x 18", 2011.
Courtesy of Mark Robbins Photography.

Cow on Right. Colored pencil on Rives BFK, 22" x 28", 2011.
Courtesy of Mark Robbins Photography.

John A. Hancock

Since 2000, I have lived, taught, and made art amid the beautiful Blue Ridge Mountains of Virginia. Prior to moving here, I resided throughout the Southeast and Midwest, from Atlanta to Wichita, from Florida to North Carolina. These places, and all my travels, have probably fueled the imagery in my art.

My paintings and drawings are the result of exploration. I want to explore the natural world and our place in it. I guess there is something of a naturalist or a natural historian in my approach. The flora and fauna, the rocks and creeks, the broad sweep of a mountain range or details of a small plant can completely capture my attention. These all end up in my paintings. As for my large drawings, well, so do echoes of family stories from those living on the land.

My work usually starts with drawing and painting outside. Later, back in the studio, I use my drawings, sketches, notes, and, yes, maybe a few photographs to create paintings in watercolor, gouache, or acrylic. Just as frequently, I use a combination of all of those and many other materials as I improvise and experiment my way through the work.

With that traditional, almost classical way of starting a work of art, you might expect me to create traditional landscape images. I do finish a few pieces as just such pure landscapes. Most of my work though also has an abstract element interjected into them. I interrupt the viewer's immediate access to the landscape by juxtaposing or layering two pictures together. Or I might float geometric shapes, maps, or diagrams into the work. Am I a modernist or a classicist? Yes, both — and with an idiosyncratic twist too.

What Answer Would Eiliesh Have Had?
Mixed media on Mylar, 86" x 30", 2006-07.

Like Descartes, A Watchful Eye. Mixed media on Mylar, 268" x 42", 2009.

Against A Winter Sky. Mixed aqueous media on panel, 12" x 12", 2008.

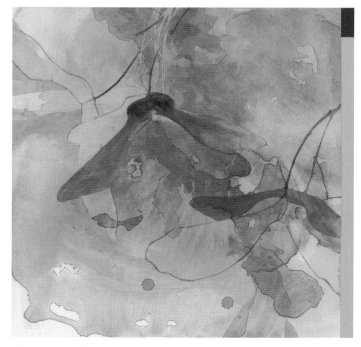

Maplewing #1. Mixed aqueous media on panel, 12" x 12", 2008.

NNW From Afton. Mixed aqueous media on panel, 12" x 12", 2010.

Ed Hatch

I strive to create a mood in my paintings that evoke a sense of place, calmness, and visual poetry. I especially enjoy painting scenes of streams and small meandering rivers. Occasionally, I paint from my canoe or skiff, and my years of experience in floating rivers have helped me to study water and portray its visual nuance. Living in Virginia, we have very humid air in the summer. I attempt to create this thickly laden atmosphere in my paintings and try to get the viewer to be drawn into the painting and participate emotionally.

I see art as a visceral, almost spiritual means of communication. Since I was a boy, I have known that art fulfills me. It speaks to me in ways that I find difficult to express in words, but what I find in nature is, quite simply, pure poetry. I strive to express this in my work. I see such extraordinary beauty in everyday moments — moments that might go unnoticed. I want people to participate in my paintings and to get caught up in the scenes. I want the viewer to feel the depth, the fleeting light, the mist, and wonder what may lie beyond. That's it, I think, to share the wonder. I find great joy in painting and feel very fortunate to make a living by following my passion for it.

Artist with *Downstream*, an oil on canvas, in the background.
Courtesy of George Laumann.

Shenandoah Scene. Oil on panel,
16" x 20", 2010.

Summer Air. Oil on panel, 24" x 36", 2010.

Old Blind. Oil on panel, 11" x 14", 2010.

Downstream. Oil on panel, 30" x 40", 2011.

Lindsey Mears

Courtesy of Stacey V. Evans.

In my artist's books, I combine layers of images with original and historic texts, to create narratives that combine the past and present. My imagery explores interactions of people and the environment, with the belief that the elements, flora, and fauna are all equal players in a narrative.

The landscape of the South is powerful; everywhere you look, things are growing and creatures are living. Even the air has weight and a palpable presence. I find comfort and connection with the past through our shared landscape. I'm interested in how aspects of the environment can signify human emotion and experience.

My work also focuses on the material environment: the everyday items we surround ourselves with. I'm drawn to the patterns and designs we share in common through time. I'm interested in exploring their relationships to the external and internal human landscape.

The aesthetic intention of my work is closely tied to process. I work in several different media; most of it based in obsolete technologies, which, by their nature, can yield unexpected results. For me, making art is a process of discovery.

Westward Expansion (cover). Artist's book with gum bichromate, chromatype, mixed media, 8" x 9" x 2.5", 2007. *Courtesy of Stacey V. Evans.*

Westward Expansion. Artist's book with gum bichromate, chromatype, mixed media, 8" x 9" x 2.5", 2007. *Courtesy of Stacey V. Evans.*

Fabre's Moth. Artist's book with bleached/toned cyanotype, letterpress text, mixed media, 9" x 8" x 1.5", 2006. *Courtesy of Stacey V. Evans.*

Abide. Artist's book with cyanotype, gum bichromate, mixed media, 5.5" x 5" x 1.25", 2009. *Courtesy of Stacey V. Evans.*

Album: Devils Pursue Her. Artist's book with bleached/toned/waxed cyanotype, gum bichromate, mixed media, 11" x 7.5" x 2.5", 2004. *Courtesy of Stacey V. Evans.*

Marcelo Novo

Like a musician playing by ear and improvising as he goes, my art begins not with cautious preliminary sketches but working directly on the chosen surface and completing the work in one sitting. When I begin, I never know what will manifest itself. I start doodling, and when I feel things are happening, I follow. I don't go back to re-work a painting, allowing for a more spontaneous and intuitive process.

My artistic roots are in Latin American and European Surrealism, a movement that believes art holds the key to unlock the inner workings of the mind and reveal aspects of the psyche otherwise hidden. Diverse recurrent symbols appear in my work as manifestations of my life experiences, some of which are closely related to my Latin American cultural heritage and my youth in Buenos Aires, Argentina.

Most of my twenty years in the United States I have spent in South Carolina, and while other art or artists there did not directly influence my art, the particular environment has pushed me to dig deeper into my own artistic world. For my recent Map Series, the chosen surface includes portions of maps from the USA and elsewhere, on which I paint instinctive/subconscious images. The appeal and use of maps relate to my travels and especially to my identity and sense of place. As I mark two decades in the United States, the imagery in my work continues to evolve, reflecting my identity in two cultures and my experience in many places.

Artist with a detail of his mural, *Hope*, 2009.

Perro Bueno. Acrylic on canvas, 40" x 30", 2010.

Picaflor. Acrylic on map on canvas, 12" x 12", 2010.

Ambiguous. Acrylic on map on canvas, 12" x 12", 2008.

Journey. Acrylic on map and stamps on canvas, 16" x 20", 2007.

Paul Reed

After working as an abstract expressionist, I began staining canvases in 1959 when water-based acrylics became available. Experimentation with the properties and effects of the new medium became central to my art. I created works with mandala shapes, biomorphic hard-edged shapes, and free, open, partly overlaying bands of colors as well as shaped, unstretched canvases directly attached to the wall.

That I lived in Washington, D.C., might have contributed to these developments; the city became a main center for color field painting, to which experimentation with acrylics was central. In the mid 1960s, I was one of six painters in the first traveling exhibition of what often is referred to as the Washington Color School. The others were Morris Louis, Kenneth Noland, Gene Davis, Howard Mehring, and Tom Downey.

Experimentation with materials, surfaces, shapes, and forms and the effects of light have been at the core of my paintings and drawings ever since. In the early 1970s, I began working with oil pastels on paper. I liked feeling the touch of the paper: the texture, the surface. I have created gouache paintings on Plexiglas transferred to paper. I made "quad" photo collages, joining two seemingly unrelated photographs and their mirror image.

In the 1990s, I went back to a very thin layering of acrylic paints and transparent glazes, at times contrasted with geometric shapes of thick paint. Subsequently, the colors became bolder, the forms more expressionistic and, working on muslin, the effects of light more pronounced. In recent years, I have experimented with paintings of thin abstract and semi-abstract forms on thin materials, placing them in windows to allow for an optimal, changing effect of natural light.

Courtesy of Ashleigh Burke Coleman.

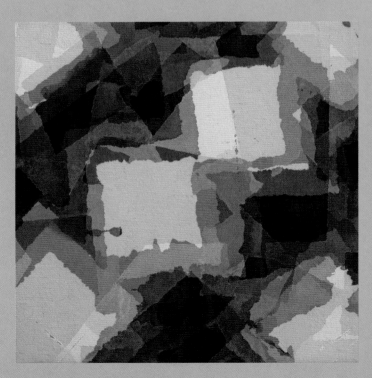

Turkoman. Acrylic on canvas, 12" x 12", 1998.
Courtesy of Ashleigh Burke Coleman.

17 DR. Acrylic on canvas, 35" x 26", 1965. *Courtesy of if ART Gallery.*

GLQ. Acrylic on muslin, 26" x 18", 2005. *Courtesy of Ashleigh Burke Coleman.*

Zig-Field. Silkscreen, 89/93, 20" x 35", 1970. *Courtesy of Ashleigh Burke Coleman.*

Tom Tombes

Courtesy of Anthony Rumley.

As an artist, I turn to my surroundings for inspiration. The rolling hills, deep rivers, blue mountains, hot beaches, dark woods, and haunting battlefields of my Virginia home provide me with a perpetual source of new ideas for paintings. My landscapes represent the patterns of the land and the water that exert their influence on my work and are a constant presence in my life.

Having been born in the swamps of Georgia, raised in the Piedmont of South Carolina and settling finally along the James River in central Virginia via New York City, I've been looking out into a southern landscape for most of my life. My great-great grandfather was mortally wounded at the battle of Frayser's Farm outside of Richmond, and his home, Beavers Hill, is still occupied by his family in Essex County. It is a rural home, as are most of the homes in the South. Many of my paintings have their roots in the rural landscapes of Virginia, and they reflect the character of the land, history, and pathos that define this region.

Southerners were the first people to sing the blues, and there is a wide streak of those dark tones in my work. The South is a brooding and mysterious place where the ghosts of war, oppression, and strife still drift by in the breeze. I employ atmospheric effects and muted tones in many of my paintings to reflect those grey areas in our history and the shadows they have cast.

Corolla. Oil on panel, 12" x 24", 2005.

Deep Garden. Oil on panel, 24" x 36", 2004.

Lower Cascade Gorge. Oil on linen, 18" x 24", 2005.

Old Friends. Oil on canvas, 20" x 36", 2007.

Buffalo Barn. Oil on wood panel, 18" x 24", 2010.

Kathleen Westkaemper

Although I was born in California, for the past thirty years I have lived in Virginia.

When I came to Richmond I was delighted to live in a part of the country with seasons, where there are real winters and springs. I particularly enjoyed the variety of birds I could see daily in my own backyard. Observing blackbirds, bluebirds, goldfinches, or chickadees out my kitchen window, I am drawn into their daily lives. I love the winters, when the trees are bare, and the branches make a poetic framework for the many birds that visit my feeder. Since childhood, I have felt the need to draw what I saw each day. Birds have figured in these drawings as long as I can remember.

Shortly after moving to Richmond, I found the Virginia Museum of Fine Arts Studio School. In a class taught by John Morgan, I discovered oil pastels and paint sticks. I have been drawing with oil pastels, paint sticks, and graphite for more than twenty years now. I begin by drawing with graphite and then blending in the paint sticks. I work directly on the paper, blending and mixing the paint sticks and graphite with my fingers. I love the immediacy of working this way, and the colors are intense and textural. I enjoy the physical process and feel that this medium is ideal for expressing the essence and emotion of the images I am compelled to put on paper.

Richmond has two universities, a remarkable art museum, and a multitude of art galleries. Since 1993 I have been an artist member of Artspace, a local nonprofit art gallery. My work has been exhibited throughout the Mid-Atlantic and has won numerous awards in regional and national shows. The vigorous art scene that exists in Richmond, Virginia, continually inspires me.

A Gathering. Paint stick and graphite on gessoed paper, 24" x 24", 2009.

Passing Blackbirds. Paint stick and graphite on gessoed paper, 24" x 24", 2010.

On the Wires. Paint stick and graphite on gessoed paper, 20" x 20", 2010.

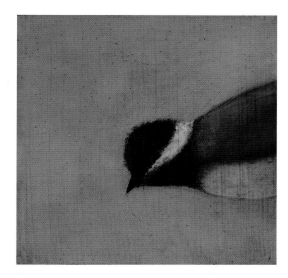

Chickadee. Paint stick and graphite on gessoed paper, 3.5" x 3.5", 2011.

Goldfinch. Paint stick and graphite on gessoed paper, 3.5" x 3.5", 2011.

Titmouse. Paint stick and graphite on gessoed paper, 3.5" x 3.5", 2011.

7.
West Virginia

Bill Hopen

I fled New York City in 1974, moving to Sutton, West Virginia (pop. 1,000). My fellow New York City artists thought me crazy to leave "the art center of the world" to go live in Appalachia. My goal was to become uncrazy — to make artworks in tranquility, surrounded by natural beauty. Perhaps I was emulating Thoreau or Emerson, seeking a simple environment of joy and serenity in which to create and inviting that serenity to enter into my artwork. I moved south and built a tiny studio in the woods and began carving wood and stone figures. As I worked at home and raised my children in this small southern community, I saw beauty clearly in the life and people here. It is that vision of the world that I strive to imbue within my figurative works; to make them affirmations of human life, its passion, its energy, its beauty, its love.

I started doing larger-than-life figures. Public art commissions and liturgical artwork assignments magically came my way, leading me to cast my works in bronze. When designing a large work, I first make a maquette, or small-scale figure study. I soon discovered a second market in these smaller works, when clients and collectors wished to acquire them. I began casting bronze and crystal editions of ninety and now devote half of my sculpting time to the creation of smaller figurative works. These works of my own personal expression are for interiors and gardens; art for "living spaces" rather than "public spaces." I love the intimate expression of a small bronze figure within a room. My smaller works, sold through the Internet, are well collected in Asia, Europe, and all over the United States.

With Speaker of the House, U.S. Senator Robert C. Byrd. *Clay of Bryd* monument is in background, maquette study to the right.

Wedding at Cana. Maquettes cast in bronze at 1/6 scale, presented 2010 to committee for approval of full-size bronze installation for Spiritual Life Center, Wichita, Kansas.

Selection of 6" bronze figures, editions of 30. *Courtesy of Jurgin Lorenzen.*

Father Du Bois. St. Mary's University, Emmitsburg, Maryland. Bronze figure with base; cross is 19' above fountain pool, 2006.

Three wax patterns, full-size figures for *Wedding at Cana,* are retouched for bronze casting, 2011.

Sister of Healing. Our Lady of the Lake Hospital, Baton Rouge, Louisiana. Bronze, 10" x 5" x 4", 1990.

Angela Lehr Bass

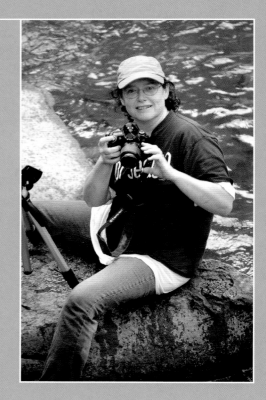

As a child, I was exposed to various types of art and woodworking. My mother is an accomplished oil painter, and my father is a wonderful pencil artist and carpenter. At the age of 10, I became passionately interested in photography. I started out with a pocket 110 camera and acquired my first 35mm for the birth of my first child in 1984. Since then, my love for photography has only increased. Living in the beautiful state of West Virginia, the incredible scenery is endless. I'm in photography heaven.

I enjoy not only capturing beautiful and breathtaking scenes, but also merging some with my other artistic skills to create unique pieces of art. My extensive background in graphic arts merges nicely with photography. I don't alter the photograph itself, but instead take elements of the photograph and enhance them with various techniques, such as the use of black and white merges, artistic borders, color muting, and other visual enhancements to create a focal point on an element of the photograph that has drawn my attention.

One of the gifts God has given me is the ability to see what often gets overlooked. I have found that many people have never noticed some of the fine details that exist all around them. Like the way a water drop holds a tiny detailed upside down image that can only be seen if you're looking. Or even what might look like a scene from another planet within the depths of a seemingly plain flower.

I take great joy in being able to expose the beauty that God has created, from my perspective, and sharing it with others. My hope is that those others will be inspired to look for the hidden beauty that's all around them, also.

Wish You Were Here. A panoramic of Sandstone Falls, 2009

Depth of Perception. A neighboring field, 2010.

Tiny World. A water drop clinging to a lilac after a rain, 2011.

New Beginnings. The last of winter, just as spring is beginning, 2009.

Amazing Iris. A macro shot of a beautiful purple iris, 2009.

Rodney LehrBass

I am not only an artist per say, more so a person who reveals the beautiful treasures God has concealed within the confines of the bark of a tree. It is my objective to uncover the natural symmetry and fascinating embellishments hidden within — deep in the core of the sweet and colorful maple, or a sturdy and robust cherry tree for instance. Gently discovering a hidden world of the "majestic" waiting to be revealed.

I gain my inspiration directly from the individual selection of wood that I have chosen to turn. I try to use local woods whenever possible. I avoid buying wood that has been forested in an unhealthy way — a way that is detrimental to our natural Appalachian wildlife territories and the abundant species of animal life that live within the wild and wonderful mountains of West Virginia; animals that rely solely on the health and wellbeing of a strong forest.

Tactile sensation is something that is very important to me. The feel and the texture of the wood play a significant role in my work, as much as the grain, color, and design itself. I believe people are drawn to a piece of art that simply says, "You've got to touch me." I prefer to accentuate the beauty of the wood's natural surface, using simple polishing techniques over the traditional use of chemical finishes whenever possible, allowing the person enjoying the piece to experience the raw natural grain and figure of the wood as God intended it to be enjoyed.

Although I often turn utilitarian pieces such as salad bowls, rolling pins, bottle stoppers and the like, my true passion lies in turning larger "natural edge" pieces of art. I find this artistic aspect of turning really fulfills my deepest hunger to turn.

The Well. A natural edge bowl turned out of maple, 2010.

Terra Majestic. A large natural edge vessel turned out of local cherry burl, 2011.

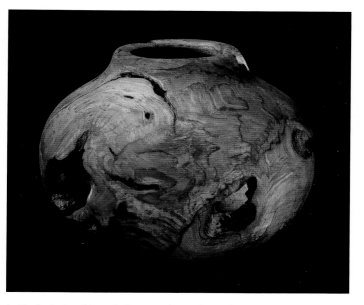

In The Beginning. A large hollow vessel turned out of maple burl, 2010.

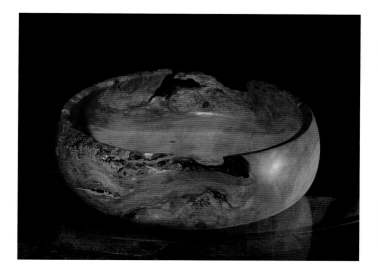

Celestial. A large natural edge trimmed bowl turned out of cherry, 2010.

Tiara. A large hollow vessel turned out of soft maple, 2009.

Where to Find the Artists

Paula Allen
Web: www.pollyzoom.com

Alice R. Ballard
Web: www.aliceballard.com
Shown at:
• Blue Spiral 1, Asheville, NC 28801
• Hodges Taylor Art Consultancy, Charlotte, NC 28202
• Tao Evolution, Hong Kong

Gwenneth Barth-White
Web: gwennethbarth.com
Shown at:
• Hughes Gallery, Boca Grande, FL 33921

Gary Bills
Web: www.BeneathTheBark.us
Shown at:
• Arrowcraft, Gatlinburg, TN 37738
• Cumberland Crafts, Middlesboro, KY 40965
• Guild Crafts, Asheville, NC 28805
• Parkway Craft Center, Blowing Rock, NC 28605

John Beard
Web: www.johnbeardfineart.com
Shown at:
• Allison Sprock Fine Art, Charleston, SC 29401
• Allison Sprock Fine Art, Charlotte, NC 28207
• Stellers Gallery, Ponte Vedra, FL 32082
• Stellers Gallery, Jacksonville, FL 32207

Carl Blair
Shown at:
• Elder Art, Charlotte, NC 28203
• Hampton III Gallery, Taylors, SC 29787
• if ART Gallery, Columbia, SC 29201

Patti Brady
Shown at:
• Frame Designs, Greenville, SC 29607
• Hodges Taylor, Charlotte, NC, 28292

Ashlynn Browning
Web: www.ashlynnbrowning.com
Shown at:
• Artspace, Raleigh, NC 27601
• Flanders Gallery, Raleigh, NC 27603
• if ART Gallery, Columbia, SC 29201

Dan Bynum
Web: danbynumart.blogspot.com
Shown at:
• Clay Scot Gallery, Birmingham, AL 35205
• Estel Gallery, Nashville, TN 37203

Betsy Cain
Shown at:
• 1704 Gallery, Savannah, GA 31401
• Kobo Gallery, Savannah, GA 31401
• Sandler-Hudson Gallery, Atlanta, GA 30318
• Williams-Cornelius Gallery, Jacksonville, FL 32204

Philip Carpenter
Shown at:
• Marcia Wood Gallery, Atlanta, GA30313

Eva Carter
Eva Carter Gallery, Charleston SC 29401
Shown at:
• Marion Meyer Contemporary Art, Laguna Beach, CA 92651

Peter A. Cerretta
Web: www.artbycerreta.com
Shown at:
• Art Affair Art Gallery, Sanford, FL 32771
• Art League of Daytona Beach, Daytona Beach, FL 32114
• Beaux Arts of Volusia, Daytona Beach, FL 32114
• Hollingsworth Art Gallery, Palm Coast, FL 32164
• James Harper Fine Art Gallery, Ormond Beach, FL 32174
• SECCA Tree Studios, Palm Coast, FL 32164

Gary Chapman
Web: www.garychapmanart.com

Delores Coe
Web: www.dolorescoe.com
Shown at:
• Allyn Gallup Contemporary Art, Sarasota, FL 34236
• Clayton Galleries, Tampa, FL 33611

Sid Daniels
Web: www.siddaniels.com
Shown at:
• Sol Gallery at Cando Arts Co-op, Miami Beach, FL 33139

Loren DiBenedetto
Web: www.lorendibenedetto.com
Shown at:
• Hughes Gallery, Boca Grande, FL 33921
• Merrill-Jennings Galleries, Davidson, NC 28036
• The Art Cellar Gallery, Banner Elk, NC 28604

Jeff Donovan
Shown at:
• if ART Gallery, Columbia, SC 29201

Christian Duran
Web: www.christianduran.com

Toni Elkins
Web: www.artistcolony.net
Web: www.watercolorusahonorsociety.org
Shown at:
• Designs By Elkins, Columbia, SC 29205

Mary Engel
Web: www.maryengel.net
Shown at:
• Marcia Wood Gallery, Atlanta, GA 30313

Bill Farnsworth
Web: www.billfarnsworth.com
Shown at:
• Courtyard Art Gallery, Mystic, CT 06355
• Elder Gallery, Charlotte, NC 28203
• John Collette Fine Art, Highlands, NC 28741
• The Hughes Gallery, Boca Grande, FL 33921

Steven Forbes-DeSoule
Shown at:
• Ariel Craft Gallery, Asheville, NC 28801
• ArtSource Fine Art, Raleigh, NC 27609
• Bella Vista Art Gallery, Asheville, NC 28803
• Carolina Clay Gallery, Johns Island, SC 2945

Charlotte Foust
Web: www.charlottefoust.com

Drew Galloway
Shown at:
• Blue Spiral 1, Asheville, NC 28801
• Fresh Paint Art Advisors, Culver City, CA 90232
• Marcia Wood Gallery, Atlanta, GA 30313
• Taylor Bercier Fine Art, New Orleans, LA 70130
• The Rymer Gallery, Nashville, TN 37219

Lilian Garcia-Roig
Web: www.liliangarcia-roig.com
Shown at:
• Blue Spiral 1 Gallery, Asheville, NC 28801
• Carol Jazzar - Contemporary Art, Miami, FL 33150
• Thomas Dean Fine Art, Atlanta, GA 30309
• Valley House Gallery, Dallas, TX 75254

Courtney Garrett
Web: www.courtneyjgarrett.com
Shown at:
• Artion Galleries, Athens, Greece
• Pryor Fine Art, Atlanta, GA 30324
• Watts Fine Art, Zionsville, IN 46077

Phil Garrett
Web: www.philgarrett.com
Shown at:
• Frame Designs Ltd, Greenville, SC 29607
• Hodges Taylor Gallery, Charlotte, NC 28202
• if ART Gallery, Columbia, SC 29201
• King Snake Press LLC, Greenville, SC 29617

Dean Gioia
Web: www.deangioia.com
Shown at:
• Monty Stabler Galleries, Homewood, AL 35209
• Strauss Gallery, Tallahassee, FL 32303
• Sutton Galleries, New Orleans, LA
• Thornebrook Gallery, Gainesville, FL 32608
• Weatherburn Gallery, Naples, FL 34102

Jeanne Goodman
Web: www.jeannegoodman.com
Shown at:
• D'art Center, Norfolk, VA 23510
• Serendip, Norfolk, VA 23510
• Soho MYRIAD, Atlanta, GA 30318A

John A. Hancock
Shown at:
• Fred Nichols Studios, Barboursville, VA 22923
• McGuffey Art Studio, Charlottesville, VA 22902

George Handy
Web: www.georgehandy.com
Shown at:
• Blue Spiral 1 Gallery, Asheville, NC

Ann Harwell
Web: www.annharwell.com
Shown at:
• Artspace, Raleigh, NC 27602
• Piedmont Craftsmen, Winston-Salem, NC 27101
• Visions Art Museum, San Diego, CA 92106

Ed Hatch
Web: www. EdHatchArt.com
Shown at:
• Brazier Fine Art, Richmond, VA 23220
• Berkley Gallery, Warrenton, VA 20186
• Greenleaf Gallery, Duck, NC 27949
• Hughes Gallery, Boca Grande, FL 33291
• McBride Gallery, Annapolis, MD 21301
• Somerville-Manning Gallery, Greenville, DE 19807
• Warm Springs Gallery, Warm Springs, VA 24484

Mana Hewitt
Shown at:
• City Art Gallery, Columbia, SC 29201
• Crimson Laurel Gallery, Bakersville, NC, 28705
• Nina Liu and Friends, Charleston, SC
• Piedmont Craftsmen Gallery, Winston-Salem, NC 27101
• Quirk Gallery, Richmond, VA 23220
• Velvet Da Vinci Gallery, San Francisco, CA 94109

Bill Hopen
Web: www.billhopen.com
Shown at:
• Bill Hopen Studio, Sutton, WV 26601

Jack Hughes
Shown at:
• Hughes Gallery, Inc., Boca Grande, FL 33921

Geoffrey Johnson
Shown at:
• Hubert Gallery, New York, NY 10075
• Principle Gallery, Alexandria, VA 22314

Jennifer J L Jones
Web: www.jenniferjljones.com
Shown at:
• Chicago Art Source Gallery, Chicago, IL 60614
• Hunter Kirkland Contemporary, Santa Fe, NM 87501
• Stellers Gallery, Ponte Vedra Beach, FL 32082

David J. Kaminsky
Web: www.davidkaminsky.com
Shown at:
• Kobo Gallery, Savannah, GA 31401
• Williams-Cornelius Gallery, Jacksonville, FL 32204

Marcus Kenney
Shown at:
• Marcia Wood Gallery, Atlanta, GA 30313

Kenson (Marbut Thompson)
Shown at:
• Pryor Fine Art, Atlanta, GA 30324

Dale Kennington
Web: www.dalekennington.com
Shown at:
• Corporate Art Source, Montgomery, AL 36106

Christy Kinard
Web: www.christykinard.com
Shown at:
• Jules Place, Boston, MA 02118
• Pryor Fine Art, Atlanta, GA 30324
• Shain Gallery, Charlotte, NC 28209

Clive King
Web: www.cliveking.org
Web: www.southernartistry.org
Web: www.drawingcenter.org

Barbara Krupp
Web: www.barbarakrupp.com
Web: www.barbarakrupp.net
Shown at:
• Dabbert Gallery, Sarasota, FL 34236
• Pennello Gallery, Cleveland, OH 44106
• Rice Gallery of Fine Art, Leawood, KS 66211

Tracey Lane
Shown at:
• Coda Gallery, Park City, UT 84060
• Gallery One, Nashville, TN 37205
• John Collette Fine Art, Highlands, NC 28741
• Jules Place, Boston, MA 02118
• Lakind Fine Art, Santa Fe, NM 87501
• Pryor Fine Art, Atlanta, GA 30324
• Studio E Gallery, Palm Beach Gardens, FL 33418

Jeffrey Lange
Web: www.langeart.com
Shown at:
• Michael Murphy Gallery, Tampa, FL 33629
• Stellers Gallery, Ponte Vedra Beach, FL 32082
• Thomas Dean Gallery, Atlanta, GA 30309

Mernet Larsen
Web: www.mernetlarsen.com
Shown at:
Vogt Gallery, New York, NY 10001

Ruth Laxon
Shown at:
• Marcia Wood Gallery, Atlanta, GA 30313
• Printed Matter, New York, NY 10011
• Vamp & Tramp, Booksellers, LLC, Birmingham, AL 35226

Angela LehrBass
Web: www.AGLart.com
Shown at:
• Carnegie Hall – Lewisburg, WV, Lewisburg, WV 24901
• Deep River Creative, Ronceverte, WV 24970
• Tamarack: The Best of West Virginia, Beckley, WV 25801

Rodney LehrBass
Web: www.HandcraftedByRodney.com
Shown at:
• Bella – The Corner Gourmet, Lewisburg, WV 24901
• Deep River Creative, Ronceverte, WV 24970
• Tamarack: The Best of West Virginia, Beckley, WV 25801

Peter Lenzo
Shown at:
• If ART Gallery, Columbia, SC 29201

Robert Levin
Web: www.robertlevin.com
Shown at:
• Blue Spiral 1 Gallery, Asheville, NC 28801
• Christa Faut Gallery, Cornelius, NC 28031
• City Art Gallery, Greenville, NC 27858
• The Collectors Gallery, Raleigh, NC 27601
• The Design Gallery, Burnsville, NC 28714
• Penland Gallery, Penland, NC 28765
• Piedmont Craftsmen Gallery, Winston Salem, NC 27101
• Prism Glass Gallery, Rockport, ME 04856
• Shine on Brightly, Asheville, NC
• Southern Highland Craft Guild Folk Art Center, Asheville, NC 28815
• Taupe Gallery, North Wilkesboro, NC 28659
• Twisted Laurel Gallery, Spruce Pine, NC 28777

Alan Loehle
Shown at:
• Marcia Wood Gallery, Atlanta, GA 30313

Lindsey Mears
Web: www.lindseymears.com
Shown at:
• McGuffey Art Center, Charlottesville, VA 22902

Tjelda vander Meijden
Web: www.tjelda.com
Web: www.tjelda.net
Web: www.palettepressprints.com
Shown at:
• Cavaliero Fine Arts, New York, NY 10018

Luisa Mesa
Shown at:
• Duane Reed Gallery, St. Louis, MO 63108

Philip Morsberger
Shown at:
• Hampton III Gallery, Taylors, SC 29787
• if ART Gallery, Columbia, SC 29201
• Valley House Gallery & Sculpture Garden, Dallas, TX 75254

Sandy Nelson
Shown at:
• ArtSource North Hills, Raleigh, NC 27609
• Elder Gallery, Charlotte, NC 28203
• Fountainside Fine Art Gallery, Wilmington, NC 28403
• Skipjack Nautical Wares and Marine Gallery, Portsmouth, VA 23704

Dorothy Netherland
Web: www.dorothynetherland.com
Shown at:
• Barbara Archer Gallery, Atlanta, GA 30307
• if ART Gallery, Columbia, SC 29201
• SCOOP Studios Contemporary Art Gallery, Charleston, SC 29401

Keith Norval
Web: www.keithnorval.com
Shown at:
• Artspace, Studio 220, Raleigh, NC 27601
• Gitana Rosa Gallery, Brooklyn, NY
• Perlow-Stevens Gallery, Columbia, MO

Marcelo Novo
Web: www.artmajeur.com/novo
Shown at:
• if ART Gallery, Columbia, SC 29201

Barbara Olsen
Web: www.barbaraolsen.com
Shown at:
• Anne Irwin Fine Art, Atlanta, GA 30306
• Bennett Gallery, Knoxville, TN 37919
• Clay Scott Gallery, Birmingham, AL 35205
• DK Gallery, Marietta, GA 30060
• Galerie Matilda, Roswell, GA 30075
• Greenleaf Gallery, Bannockburn, IL 60016

Janet Orselli
Web: www.janetorselli.com
Web: www.saatchionline.com/Orselli
Shown at:
• if Art Gallery, Columbia, SC 29201
• OK Harris, New York, NY 10012

Penny Overcash
Web: www.overcashstudios.com
Shown at:
• Andre Christine Gallery, Mooresville NC
• Xanadu Gallery, Scottsdale, AZ 85251

Matt Overend
Shown at:
• if ART Gallery, Columbia, SC 29201 Jan

Jan Clayton Pagratis
Shown at:
• Chroma Gallery, Savannah, GA 31401

Roger Palmer
Web: www.rogerclaypalmer.com
Shown at:
• Marcia Wood Gallery, Atlanta, GA 30313
• Mindy Solomon Gallery, St. Petersburg, FL 33701

Tere Pastoriza
Shown at:
• Diaspora Vibe Gallery, Miami, FL 33136

John Douglas Powers
Web: www.john-powers.com

Susie Pryor
Shown at:
• Pryor Fine Art, Atlanta, GA 30324

Paul Reed
Shown at:
• if ART Gallery, Columbia, SC 29201

Myrna Reiss
Web: myrnapottery.webs.com
Shown at:
• M R Pottery, Mooresville, NC 28117

Edward Rice
Web: www.edwardriceart.com
Shown at:
• Barbara Archer Gallery, Atlanta, GA 30307
• Greg Thompson Fine Art, North Little Rock, AR 72114
• Hampton III Gallery, Taylors, SC 29787
• if ART Gallery, Columbia, SC 29201
• Mary Pauline Projects, Augusta, GA 30901

Barbara Rivera
Shown at:
• Mauricio Padilla Gallery, Coconut Grove, FL 33133

Mark Rutkowski
Shown at:
• Effusion Gallery, Miami Beach, FL 33139
• Mark Rutkowski Fine Art, Miami Beach, FL 33139

Morgan Santander
Shown at:
• Chroma Gallery, Savannah, GA 31401

Mary Ann Scherr
Shown at:
- Collectors Gallery, Raleigh, NC 27615
- Mobilia Gallery, Cambridge, MA 02138
- Penland Gallery, Penland, NC 28765
- Visual Art Exchange. Raleigh, NC 27601

Kim Schuessler
Web: www.kimschuessler.com
Shown at:
- Pryor Fine Art, Atlanta, GA 30324
- Shain Fine Art, Charlotte, NC 28209
- Studio E, Palm Beach Gardens, FL 33418

Virginia Scotchie
Web: www.virginiascotchie.com
Shown at:
- Blue Spiral Gallery, Asheville, NC 28801
- Goldesberry Gallery, Houston, TX 77098
- Hodges Taylor Gallery, Charlotte, NC 28202
- Penland Gallery, Penland, NC 28765

Ebeth Scott-Sinclair
Web: www.ebethscottsinclair.com
Shown at:
- Hughes Gallery, Boca Grande, FL 33921
- Monty Stabler Galleries, Homewood, AL 35209

Jerry Siegel
Shown at:
- Barbara Archer Gallery, Atlanta, GA 30307
- Jennifer Hunt Gallery, Birmingham, AL
- Rebekah Jacob Gallery, Charleston, SC 29401

Laura Spong
Shown at:
- Hampton III Gallery, Taylors, SC 29787
- if ART Gallery, Columbia, SC 29201

Katherine Taylor
Shown at:
- Marcia Wood Gallery, Atlanta, GA 30313

Pringle Teetor
Web: www.flambeauxart.com
Shown at:
- Cedar Creek Gallery, Creedmoor, NC 27522
- FRANK, Chapel Hill, NC 27514
- Hillsborough Gallery of Arts, Hillsborough, NC 27278
- North Carolina Crafts Gallery, Carrboro, NC 27510

W. Gerome Temple
Shown at:
- Chroma Gallery, Savannah, GA 31401

Dayna Thacker
Web: www.daynathacker.com
Shown at:
- Barbara Archer Gallery, Atlanta, GA 30307
- Wally Workman Gallery, Austin, TX 78703

Claudia Gibson Thomas
Web: www.Claudiathomas.nobullart.com
Shown at:
- Art Affair Gallery, Sanford, FL 32771
- Gallery at Avalon Island, Orlando, FL 32801

Tom Tombes
Shown at:
- Glave Kocen Gallery, Richmond, VA 23220
- The Gallery at Merchant's Square, Williamsburg, VA 23185

Matt Toole
Shown at:
- Chroma Gallery, Savannah, GA 31401

Leo Twiggs
Web: www.leotwiggs.com
Shown at:
- Hampton III Gallery, Taylors, SC 29787
- if ART Gallery, Columbia, SC 29201

Mary Walker
Web: www.marywalkerart.com
Shown at:
- Corrigan Gallery, Charleston, SC 29401
- Julie Heller Gallery, Provincetown, MA 02657
- Mary Praytor Gallery, Greenville, SC 29601

Kathleen Westkaemper
Web: www.kathleenwestkaemper.com
Shown at:
- Artspace, Richmond, VA 23224
- Crossroads Art Center, Richmond, VA 23230
- Glave Kocen Gallery, Richmond, VA 23220

Enid Williams
Web: www.enidwilliams.net
Shown at:
- Artizen Fine Arts, Dallas, TX 75207
- Marji Gallery & Contemporary Projects, Santa Fe, NM 87501

Mike Williams
Web: www.mikewilliamsart.com
Shown at:
- Cheryl Newby Gallery, Pawleys Island, SC 29585
- if ART Gallery, Columbia, SC 29201

David H. Yaghjian
Web: http://sites.google.com/site/dyaghjian/home
Shown at:
- if ART Gallery, Columbia, SC 29201
- Vision Gallery, Atlantic Beach, NC 28512

Paul Yanko
Web: www.paulyanko.net
Shown at:
- Hampton III Gallery, Taylors, SC 29687
- if ART Gallery, Columbia, SC 29201
- Marji Gallery & Contemporary Projects, Santa Fe, NM 87501
- Water Street Gallery, Douglas, MI 49406

Linda S. Young
Web: mspie21@comcast.net
Web: www.lindasyoung.com
Shown at:
- Art & Soul, Myrtle Beach, SC, 29577
- Gallery 333, North Falmouth, MA 02556
- Sunset River Marketplace, Calabash, NC, 28467
- Watershed Gallery, Cataumet, MA 02534

Don Zurlo
Web: www.donzurlo.com
Shown at:
- if ART Gallery, Columbia, SC 29201

Galleries & Museums

Alabama
• *Clay Scot Gallery*
2915 Highland Avenue
Birmingham, AL 35205
www.clayscot.com
• *Corporate Art Source*
2960 Zelda Road
Montgomery, AL 36106
• *Jennifer Hunt Gallery*
2800 Cahata Village Plaza
Birmingham, AL 35243
www.jenniferhuntgallery.com
• *Monty Stabler Galleries*
1811 29th Avenue South
Homewood, AL 35209
www.montystablergalleries.com
• *Vamp & Tramp, Booksellers, LLC*
South Hall Building
1951 Hoover Court, Suite 205
Birmingham, AL 35226
www.vampandtramp.com

Arizona
• *Xanadu Gallery*
7039 E. Main Street, #101
Scottsdale AZ 85251
ww.xanadugallery.com

Arkansas
• *Greg Thompson Fine Art*
429 Main Street
North Little Rock, AR 72114
www.gregthompsonfineart.com

California
• *Fresh Paint Art Advisors*
9355 Culver Boulevard, Ste. B
Culver City, CA 90232
www.freshpaintart.com
• *Marion Meyer Contemporary Art*
354 North Coast Highway
Laguna Beach CA 92651
www.MarionMeyerGallery.com
• *Velvet Da Vinci Gallery*
2015 Polk Street
San Francisco, CA 94109
www.velvetdavinci.com
• *Visions Art Museum*
2825 Dewey Road
San Diego, CA 92106

Connecticut
• *Courtyard Art Gallery*
12 Water Street, Suite B4
Mystic, CT 06355
www.courtyardgallerymystic.com

Delaware
• *Somerville-Manning Gallery*
Brecks Mill, 2nd Floor
101 Stone Block Row
Greenville, DE 19807
www.somervillemanning.com

Florida
• *Allyn Gallup Contemporary Art*
1288 North Palm Avenue
Sarasota, FL 34236
www.allyngallup.com
• *Art Affair Gallery*
303 East First St.
Sanford, FL 32771
www.artaffairgallery.com
• *Art League of Daytona Beach*
433 South Palmetto
Daytona Beach, FL 32114
www.itsmysite.com
• *Beaux Arts of Volusia*
433 South Palmetto
Daytona Beach, FL 32114
www.itsmysite.com/beauxarts
• *Carol Jazzar - Contemporary Art*
158 NW 91 Street
Miami, FL 33150
305-490-6906
www.cjazzart.com
• *Clayton Galleries*
4105 South MacDill Avenue
Tampa, FL 33611
www.claytongalleries.net
• *Dabbert Gallery*
76 South Palm Avenue
Sarasota, Florida 34236
www.dabbertgallery.com
• *Diaspora Vibe Gallery*
3938 North Miami Avenue
Miami, FL 33136
www.diasporavibe.net
• *Effusion Gallery*
1130 Ocean Drive

Miami Beach, FL 33139
www.effusiongallery.com
• *Gallery at Avalon Island*
39 South Magnolia Avenue
Orlando, FL 32801
www.galleryatavalonisland.com
• *Hollingsworth Art Gallery*
160 Cypress Point Parkway
Suites 209B & 210B
Palm Coast, FL 32164
www.hollingsworth.com
• *Hughes Gallery*
333 Park Avenue
Boca Grande, FL 33921
www.hughesgallery.net
• *James Harper Fine Art Gallery*
44 West Granada Boulevard
Ormond Beach, FL 32174
www.jhfinearts.com
• *Mindy Solomon Gallery*
124 2nd Avenue NE
St. Petersburg, FL 33701
www.mindysolomon.com
• *Mark Rutkowski Fine Art*
405 Espanola Way
Miami Beach, FL 33139
www.MarkRutkowski.com
• *Mauricio Padilla Gallery*
2200 South Dixie Highway, Ste. 704
Coconut Grove, FL 33133
www.mauriciopadilla.com
• *Michael Murphy Gallery*
2701 South MacDill
Tampa, FL 33629
www.michaelmurphygallery.com
• *Permanent Collection at the Heritage Center*
642 West New England Avenue
Winter Park, FL 32789
www.hannibalsquareheritagecenter.org
• *SECCA Tree Studios*
160 Cypress Point Parkway
Suite 208
Palm Coast, FL 32164
www.hollingsworth.com
• *Sol Gallery at Cando Arts Co-op*
309 23rd Street
Miami Beach, FL 33139
www.solgallerymiamibeach.com
• *Stellers Gallery*
240 A1a N # 13

Ponte Vedra, FL 32082
stellersgallery.com
and 1409 Atlantic Boulevard
Jacksonville, FL 32207
• *Strauss Gallery*
1950 Thomasville Road
Tallahassee, FL 32303
• *Studio E Gallery*
PGA Commons East
4600 PGA Boulevard, Suite 101
Palm Beach Gardens, FL 33418
www.studioegallery.com
• *Thornebrook Gallery*
2441 Northwest 43rd Street, #6D,
Gainesville, FL 32608
www.thornebrookgallery.com
• *Weatherburn Gallery*
452 Bayfront Place
Naples, FL 34102
www.weatherburn.com
• *Williams-Cornelius Gallery*
643 Edison Avenue
Jacksonville, FL 32204
www.williamscornelius.com

Georgia
• *1704 Gallery*
1704 Lincoln Street
Savannah, GA 31401
www.1704lincoln.com
• *Anne Irwin Fine Art*
25-D Bennett Street
Atlanta, GA 30306
www.anneirwinfineart.com
• *Barbara Archer Gallery*
280 Elizabeth Street, #A012
Atlanta, GA 30307
www.barbaraarcher.com
• *DK Gallery*
25 West Park Square
Marietta, GA 30060
www.dkgallery.us
• *Galerie Matilda*
959 Canton Street
Roswell, GA 30075
www:galeriematilda.com
• *Kobo Gallery*
33 Barnard Street
Savannah, GA 31401
• *Marcia Wood Gallery*
263 Walker Street SW
Atlanta, GA 30313
www.marciawoodgallery.com
• *Mary Pauline Projects*
965 Broad Street
Augusta, GA 30901

404-272-7390
www.marypaulineprojects.com
• *Pryor Fine Art*
764 Miami Circle
Atlanta, GA 30324
www.pryorfineart.com
• *Sandler-Hudson Gallery*
1009 Marietta Street Northwest
Atlanta, GA 30318
www.sandlerhudson.com
• *Soho MYRIAD*
1250 Menlo Drive NW
Atlanta, GA 30318
• *Thomas Dean Fine Art*
22-B Bennett Street
Atlanta, GA 30309
404-352-3778
www.thomasdeans.com

Illinois
• *Chicago Art Source Gallery*
1871 N. Clybourn Avenue
Chicago IL 60614
www.chicagoartsource.com
• *Greenleaf Gallery*
1760 Sunset Lane
Bannockburn, IL 60016
www.greenleafgallery.com

Indiana
• *Watts Fine Art*
20 N. Main Street
Zionsville, IN 46077
www.wattsfineart.com

Kansas
• *Rice Gallery of Fine Art*
11535 Ash Street
Leawood, KS 66211
www.thericegallery.com

Kentucky
• *Cumberland Crafts*
US 25E
Middlesboro, KY 40965

Louisiana
• *Sutton Galleries*
519 Royal Street
New Orleans, LA 70130
• *Taylor Bercier Fine Art*
233 Chartres Street
New Orleans, LA 70130
www.taylorbercier.com

Maine
• *Prism Glass Gallery*
297 Commercial St.
Rockport, ME 04856
www.prismglassgallery.com

Maryland
• *McBride Gallery*
215 Main Street
Annapolis, MD 24401
www.mcbridegallery.com

Massachusetts
• *Gallery 333*
333 Old Main Road
North Falmouth, MA 02556
www.gallery333.com
• *Jules Place*
1200 Washington Street, #204
Boston, MA 02118
www.julesplace.com
• *Julie Heller Gallery*
2 Gosnold Street
Provincetown, MA 02657
www.juliehellergallery.com
• *Mobilia Gallery*
258 Huron Avenue
Cambridge, MA 02138
www.Mobilia-Gallery.com
• *Watershed Gallery*
Kingman Yacht Center
Cataumet, MA 02534

Michigan
• *Water Street Gallery*
98 Center Street
Douglas, MI 49406
www.waterstreetgallery.com

Missouri
• *Duane Reed Gallery*
4729 McPherson Avenue
St. Louis, MO 63108
www.duanereedgallery.com
• *Perlow-Stevens Gallery*
1025 East Walnut Street
Columbia, MO 65201
www.perlow-stevensgallery.com

New Mexico
• *Hunter Kirkland Contemporary*
200-B Canyon Road
Santa Fe, NM 87501
www.hunterkirklandcontemporary.com
• *Lakind Fine Art*
662 Canyon Road

Santa Fe, NM 87501
www.lakindfineart.com
• *Marji Gallery & Contemporary Projects*
217 Water Street
Santa Fe, NM 87501
www.marjigallerysantafe.com

New York
• *Cavaliero Fine Arts*
580 Eighth Avenue, 4th Floor
New York, NY 10018
www.cavalierofinearts.com
• *Gitana Rosa Gallery*
19 Hope Street
Brooklyn, NY 11211
Vanessa@gitanarosa.com
• *Hubert Gallery*
1046 Madison Ave.
New York, NY 10075
info@hubertgallery.com
• **OK Harris**
383 West Broadway
New York, NY 10012
www.okharris.com
• *Printed Matter*
195 10th Ave.
New York, NY 10011
www.printedmatter.org
• *Vogt Gallery*
508-526 West 26 Street, #91
New York, NY 10001
www.vogtgallery.com

North Carolina
• *Allison Sprock Fine Art*
600 Queens Road
Charlotte, NC 28207
• *Andre Christine Gallery*
148 Ervin Road
Mooresville, NC 28117
• *Ariel Craft Gallery*
19 Biltmore Avenue
Asheville, NC 28801
www.arielcraftgallery.com
• *ArtSource North Hills*
4351-101 The Circle at North Hills Street
Raleigh, NC 27609
www.artsource-raleigh.com
• *Bella Vista Art Gallery*
14 Lodge Street
Asheville, NC 28803
www.bellavistaart.com
• *Bloom 291 Gallery*
815 Burke Street
Winston-Salem, NC 27101
• *Blue Spiral 1*

38 Biltmore Avenue
Asheville, NC 28801
www.bluespiral1.com
• *Cedar Creek Gallery*
1150 Fleming Road
Creedmoor, NC 27522
www.cedarcreekgallery.com
• *Christa Faut Gallery*
19818 North Cove Road
Cornelius, NC 28031
www.christafautgallery.com
• *City Art Gallery*
511 Red Banks Road
Greenville, NC 27858
www.city-art-gallery.com
• *Collectors Gallery*
443 Fayetteville Street
Raleigh, NC 27615
ww.thecollectorsgallery.com
• *Crimson Laurel Gallery*
23 Crimson Laurel Way
Bakersville, NC 28705
www.Crimsonlaurelgallery.com
• *Elder Gallery*
1427 South Boulevard, Ste. 101
Charlotte, NC 28203
www.elderart.com
• *Fine Art Gallery*
4351-101 The Circle at North Hills Street
Raleigh, NC 27609
www.Artsource-raleigh.com
• *Flanders Gallery*
302 S. West Street
Raleigh, NC 27603
www.flandersartgallery.com
• *Fountainside Fine Art Gallery*
1900 Eastwood Road, Ste. 44
Wilmington, NC 28403
www.fountainsidegallery.com
• *FRANK*
109 East Franklin Street
Chapel Hill, NC 27514
www.frankisart.com
• *Greenleaf Gallery*
1169 Duck Road
Duck, NC 27949
www.outer-banks.com/greenleaf
• *Guild Crafts*
930 Tunnel Road
Asheville, NC 28805
• *Hillsborough Gallery of Arts*
121 N. Churton Street
Hillsborough, NC 27278
www.hillsboroughgallery.com
• *Hodges Taylor Gallery*
401 North Tryon

Charlotte, NC 28202
www.hodgestaylor.com
• *John Collette Fine Art*
381 Main Street
Highlands NC 28741
www.johncollettefineart.com
• *Merrill-Jennings Galleries*
463 South Main Street
Davidson, NC 28036
www.merrilljennings.com
• *M R Pottery*
149 Cypress Landing Drive
Mooresville, NC 28117
• *North Carolina Crafts Gallery*
212 W. Main Street
Carrboro, NC 27510-2082
www.nccraftsgallery.com
• *Parkway Craft Center*
Milepost 294
Blue Ridge Parkway
Blowing Rock, NC 28605
• *Penland Gallery*
3135 Conley Ridge Road
Penland, NC 28765
www.penland.org
• *Piedmont Craftsmen Gallery*
601 North Trade Street
Winston Salem, NC 27101
www.Piedmontcraftsmen.org
• *Shain Fine Art*
2823 Selwyn Avenue
Charlotte, NC 28209
www.shaingallery.com
• *Shine on Brightly*
387 Stratford Road
Asheville, NC 28814
www.shineonbrightly.com
• *Southern Highland Craft Guild*
Folk Art Center
PO Box 9545
Asheville, NC 28815
www.southernhighlandguild.org
• *Sunset River Marketplace*
10283 Beach Drive SW
Calabash, NC 28467
www.sunsetrivermarketplace.com
• *The Art Cellar Gallery*
920 Shawneehaw Avenue, Hwy 184
Banner Elk, NC 28604
www.artcellaronline.com
• *The Collectors Gallery*
443 Fayetteville Street
Raleigh, NC 27601
www.thecollectorsgallery.com
• *The Design Gallery*
7 S. Main Street

Burnsville, NC 28714
www.the-design-gallery.com
• *Taupe Gallery*
807A Main Street
North Wilkesboro, NC 28659
Taupe Gallery Facebook page
• *Twisted Laurel Gallery*
333 Locust Street
Spruce Pine, NC 28777
www.insidenc.com/mountain/twistedlaurel.
    htm
• *Vision Gallery*
407 Atlantic Beach Causeway, # 6-A
Atlantic Beach, NC 28512
www.twogalleries.net
• *Visual Art Exchange*
323 Blake Street
Raleigh NC 27601

Ohio

• *Pennello Gallery*
12407 Mayfield Road
Cleveland, OH 44106
www.pennellogallery.com

South Carolina

• *Allison Sprock Fine Art*
179 1/2 King Street
Charleston, SC 29401
• *Art & Soul*
5001 N. Kings Highway, Ste. 105
Rainbow Harbor
Myrtle Beach, SC 29577
www.artandsoulmb.com
• *Carolina Clay Gallery*
565 Freshfields Drive
Johns Island, SC 2945
www.carolinaclaygallery.com
• *Cheryl Newby Gallery*
PO Box 3169
11096 Ocean Highway
Pawleys Island, SC 29585
www.cherylnewbygallery.com
• *City Art Gallery*
1224 Lincoln Street
Columbia, SC 29201
www.Cityartonline.com
• *Corrigan Gallery*
62 Queen Street
Charleston, SC 29401
www.corrigangallery.com
• *Eva Carter Gallery*
6 Gillion Street, Suite 8
Charleston SC 29401
www.EvaCarter.com
• *Designs By Elkins*

1511 Adger Road
Columbia, SC 29205
• *Frame Designs*
1322 E Washington Street, # B1
Greenville, SC 29607-1867
www.framedesignsedhouse.com
• *Hampton III Gallery*
3110 Wade Hampton Boulevard
Taylors, SC 29787
www.hamptoniiigallery.com
• *if ART Gallery*
1223 Lincoln Street
Columbia, SC 29201
www.ifartgallery.blogspot.com
• *King Snake Press LLC*
131 Woodland Drive
Greenville, SC 29617
• *Mary Praytor Gallery*
26 S Main Street
Greenville, SC 29601
www.themarypraytorgallery.com
• *Nina Liu and Friends*
24 State Street
Charleston, SC
• *Rebekah Jacob Gallery*
169-B King Street
Charleston, SC 29401
www.rebekahjacobgallery.com
• *SCOOP Studios Contemporary Art Gallery*
57-1/2 Broad Street
Charleston, SC 29401
www.scoopcontemporary.com

Tennessee

• *Arrowcraft*
576 Parkway
Gatlinburg, TN 37738
• *Bennett Gallery*
5308 Kingston Pike
Knoxville, TN 37919
www.bennettgalleries.com
• *Estel Gallery*
115 Rosa Parks Boulevard
Nashville, TN 37203
www.estelgallery.com
• *Gallery One*
5133 Harding Pike
Suite 1A
Nashville, TN 37205
www.galleryone.biz
• *Shain Gallery*
2823 Selwyn Avenue, #K
Charlotte, NC 28209
www.shaingallery.com
• *The Rymer Gallery*
233 5th Avenue N

Nashville, TN 37219
www.therymergallery.com

Texas

• *Artizen Fine Arts*
1231 Dragon Street
Dallas, TX 75207
www.artizenfinearts.com
• *Goldesberry Gallery*
2625 Colquitt
Houston, TX 77098
www.goldesberrygallery.com
• *Valley House Gallery*
6616 Spring valley Road
Dallas, TX 75254
www.valleyhouse.com
• *Wally Workman Gallery*
1202 West 6th Street
Austin, TX 78703
www.wallyworkmangallery.com

Utah

• *Coda Gallery*
804 Main Street
Park City, UT 84060
www.codagallery.com

Virginia

• *Artspace*
0 East Fourth Street
Richmond, VA 23224
www.artspacegallery.org
• *Brazier Fine Art*
1616 W. Main Street
Richmond, VA 23220
www.brazierstudio.com
• *Berkley Gallery*
40 Main Street
Warrenton, VA 20186
www.berkleygallery.com
• *Crossroads Art Center*
2016 Staples Mill Road
Richmond, VA 23230
www.crossroadsartcenter.com
• *D'art Center*
Selden Arcade
208 East Main Street
Norfolk, VA 23510
• *Fred Nichols Studio*
5420 Governor Barbour Street
Barboursville, VA 22923
fred@frednichols.com
• *Glave Kocen Gallery*
1620 West Main Street
Richmond, VA 23220
www.glavekocengallery.com

Bibliography

Paula Allen
Catskill Writers and Artists: Outside the Catskills and Beyond. Treadwell, New York: Bright Hill Press, 1997.
Multiple Authors, *Lake George Arts Project Literary Review, Vol. II, No. 1*. Lake George, New York: Lake George Arts Project, Inc., 1995.

Gwenneth Barth-White
Canterbury, Jessica. "Gwenneth Barth-White." *The Pastel Journal*, April 2011, p. 50.
Delfosse, Annie. "Gwenneth Barth et le portrait." *Dessin et Peinture: Spécial Portraits*. April-May 2006, pp. 12-15.
"Gwenneth Barth." *International Artist Magazine*, October 2000, pp. 114-121.

Alice R. Ballard
American Ceramic Society. "Studio Ceramics – Advanced Techniques." *Ceramic Arts Handbook Series, Alice Ballard's Pod Series*.
Ariail, Kate Dobbs. "Review." *American Craft*, February/March 2006.
"Design Inspiration Guide: Plants." Asheville, North Carolina: Lark Books Publication, 2011.
Hicks, Ann. *Greenville Talk Magazine*, February 2011.
Mathieson, John. *Techniques Using Slips*. Philadelphia, Pennsylvania: University of Pennsylvania Press, 2010.
Schultz, Katey. "Expecting Wonders: Alice Ballard's Pod Series." *Ceramics Monthly*, Vol. 57, Issue 4, April 2009; pp. 38-39.
Scotchie, Virginia. "Setting up Your Ceramic Studio," *Handbuilder's Atelier*. Asheville, North Carolina: Lark Publishing Company, 2003.

Carl Blair
Blair, Carl R., Wim Roefs and Leo Twiggs. "A Collection for Margaret: The Private and Personal Art of Carl R. Blair." Greenville, SC: Hampton III Gallery, 2006.
Bodine, William B., Jr. "Carl R. Blair: The Patterned Landscape." Columbia, South Carolina: Columbia Museum of Art, 2001.
"Carl Blair: Old & New/Anna Redwine." Columbia, South Carolina: if ART Gallery, 2007.
Roefs, Wim. "Carl Blair: The Verner Award Celebration Exhibition." Columbia, SC: if ART, International Fine Art Services & Lewis & Clark Gallery, 2005.

Patti Brady
"Brady Evokes a Sense of Color." *Greenville News*, August 2001.
"Garden State." *Artist's Magazine*, July 2007.

Ashlynn Browning
Amenoff, Gregory. "Joan Mitchell Foundation MFA Recipients Exhibition." New York, New York: CUE Art Foundation (Exhibition catalogue essay), June 2004.
Lassiter, Joie. "Surface Matters." Exhibition catalogue. Charlotte, North Carolina, February 2004.
Stoddard, Leah. "Tangible Gestures." Exhibition catalogue. Raleigh, North Carolina, November 2007.
Zevitas, Steven, ed. *New American Paintings: Juried Exhibition-in-Print, Vol. 82*. Ron Platt, curator. Boston, Massachusetts: Open Studios Press, June 2009.

Betsy Cain
"Beyond the Gift of Time, Current Work by Fellows of the Roswell Artist-in-Residence Program." Catalog. Roswell Museum and Art Center. Roswell, New Mexico: May 2008.
"In situ." Solo Exhibition. Catalog. Jepson Center for the Arts, Savannah, Georgia: 2011.
"The Painter's Reel, Contemporary Painting in GA." Catalog. Macon Museum of Arts and Sciences. Macon, Georgia: January 2009.

Philip Carpenter
"Past and Present: GA Museum Spotlights Six Artists, Then and Now." *Atlanta Journal Constitution*, Aug. 2, 2002; p. 6.
"Philip Carpenter." *Art Papers*, September - October 2002; p. 41.
"Philip Carpenter." *New American Paintings, Number 52*, June 2004; pp. 22-25.
"Play: A Group Show at Spruill Gallery." Burnaway.org. April 1, 2009.
"Tool Time." *Creative Loafing*, February 24 - March 4, 2005; p. 49.

Eva Carter
Hallsten McGarry, Susan. "Awakened Memories." *Focus/Santa Fe*, January 2005.
Harvin, Stephanie. "High Profile." *The Post and Courier*, January 3, 2003.
Huggins, Stacy. "Artist Profile: Eva Carter." *Charleston Art Magazine*, Spring 2011.
Indyke, Dottie. "Reviews: National; Eva Carter, Joyce Robbins, Santa Fe." *Art News*, December 2004.
Kutkus, Kristina. *Eva Carter Paintings & Monotypes*. Charleston, SC: Gibbes Museum of Art Press, 1993.

Mooney, Linda. "Expressions of the Soul." *Charleston Style and Design*, Fall 2008.

Phillips, Ted. "Forces of Nature." *Charleston Magazine*, September/October 2001.

Peter Cerretta

Aumann, Tiffany. "Artist of the Year Makes You Think." *Flagler/Palm Coast Community Times*, Nov. 2000; p. 1.

Brook, Carla. Staff. "Local Artist Peter Cerreta Featured in St. Augustine." *Flagler/Palm Coast News Tribune*, December 2005; p. 5.

"Prolific Artist Find Happiness Teaching Others." *Flagler/Palm Coast News Tribune*, July 2002; p. 5.

Chadbourn, Jessica. "Artist's Work True Human Interest." *Flagler/Palm Coast News Tribune*, Sept. 1996; p. 4.

Fortier, Shanna. "Palm Coast's GOLA (gallery of local art) Artist of the Month." *Palm Coast Courier*, January 2011; p. 20.

Garret, Betty. "Minimalists Sculpture." *Flagler/Palm Coast News Tribune*, May 2000; p. 4.

Moore, Robin. "Peter Cerreta Named Art League of Daytona: Artist in Residence." *Art League of Daytona Journal*, May 2011; p. 1.

Mullen, Sandy. "Peter Cerreta - Art Meets Technology - A 21st Century Marriage." *Flagler Magazine*, Summer 2004; pp. 34-35.

Russo, Harry. "Sculpture Carries Life Philosophies." *Daytona Beach Community College Journal*, October 1989; p. 7.

Shaw, Mary. "Arts Alive, A Little Art with Your Shrimp." *The Sanford Herald*, April 2010; p. 3.

Volpe, Arlene. "Forsaken in the USA." *Palm Coast Courier*, Oct. 2005; pp. 14-15.

Gary Chapman

"American Paintings: From the Montgomery Museum of Fine Arts," 2006; pp. 14, 248, 249, & 260.

"Celebrating Contemporary Art in Alabama: The Nature of Being Southern," Art Time Studios exhibition catalog; pp. 22-23.

Clark, Georgine, ed. "Alabama Masters: Artists and Their Work." The Alabama State Council on The Arts, supported by an American Masterpieces Award from the National Endowment for the Arts; pp. 22-23.

Kemper Museum of Contemporary Art; Kansas City, Missouri; pp. 38-41.

"New American Paintings, Book 88." Needham, Massachusetts: The Open Studios Press. Juried by Barbara O'Brien, Curator. 2010.

Delores Coe

"Dolores Coe." *SAW PALM – Florida Literature and Art Journal*, Spring 2009; pp. 50-52, cover.

"Dolores Coe: Window to her World." *Flair Magazine*, Spring 2007; pp. 55-59.

"Layers: Between Science and the Imagination." ART PAPERS. Exhibition Review. March/April 1998.

"Natural Histories." ART PAPERS. Exhibition Review, January 1995.

Sid Daniels

Dawber, Martin. *Great Big Book of Fashion Illustration*. London, United Kingdom: Anova Books, 2011.

Jamieson, Laura. "Flamingos Take Flight." Where-Magazine.com, 2002.

Moore, Irene. "Art That Sizzles." Where-Magazine.com, 2004.

"Sid Daniels." *New Art Examiner*, 1981.

Taback, Simms. "Sid Daniels." *The New Illustration*, 1985.

Updike, John. "Sid Daniels." *The Art of Mickey Mouse*, 1991.

Jeff Donovan

Roefs, Wim. "Jeff Donovan: Three Decades/Twenty Years." Columbia, South Carolina: if ART Gallery, 2010.

"Construction Crew III: Steven Chapp, Jeff Donovan, Janet Orselli & Edward Rice." Columbia, South Carolina: if ART Gallery. 2007.

"Humans: Jeff Donovan, John Monteith, Dorothy Netherland & Herb Parker." Columbia, South Carolina: if ART, International Fine Art Services, 2006.

"South Carolina Birds: A Fine Arts Exhibition." Sumter, South Carolina: Sumter Gallery of Art, 2004.

Christian Duran

Clemence, Paul and Julie Davidow. *Miami Contemporary Artists*. Atglen, PA: Schiffer Publishing Ltd., 2008.

Luis, Carlos M. "Las Visiones Metaforicas de Christian Duran." *El Nuevo Herald*, April 26, 2009; p. 6D.

New American Paintings 76. South End, Massachusetts: Open Studio Press, 2008.

Trelles, Emma. "Devine Inspiration." *The Sun Sentinel*, April 12, 2009; p. 3G, 12G.

Toni Elkins

Cochan, Pat. Southwestern Watercolor Society Profiles." *The Scene Magazine*, 1996.

Krantz, Les. The New York Art Review, 1989.

"Master Painters of North America." *International Art Magazine*, 1998.

Who's Who in American Art, 2007.

Mary Engel

Acosta, Kelly. "Urban Renewal." *Southern Distinction*, October 2005.

Cullum, Jerry. "Canine companions in the garden." *Atlanta Journal-Constitution*, December 2004.

Fox, Catherine. "Animal behavior unleashed." *Access Atlanta*, January 2005.

Hammes, Mary Jessica. "Earth Transformed." *Athens Banner-Herald Daily News*, May 2000.

Jones, Janet Kendall. "Inspiration, Passion, and Nature in Clay." *Mountain Life*, May/June 2003.

Link, Melissa. "Mary Engel's creative canines." *Athens Magazine*, October 2002.

Mann, Allyson. "Dog's Are This Artist's Best Friend." *GA Magazine*, December 2004.

Roberts, Carolanne Griffith. "Doggone Art." *Southern Living*, October 2005.

Woo, Cameron. "Two artists recycle everyday objects into Sculpture." *BARK*. Berkeley, California; Fall 2005.

Steven Forbes-deSoule

Clark, Donald A. *Making a Living in Crafts*. Asheville, North Carolina: Lark Books, 2006; pp. 84-86.

Davis, Don. *Wheel Thrown Ceramics*. Asheville, North Carolina: Lark Books, 1998; pp. 112-115.

Forbes-deSoule, Steven. "Ceramics Monthly." May 1985; pp. 44-45.

"Chaos Theory." *Carolina Homes and Garden*, Spring 2009.

Hopper, Robin. "Clay and Glazes for the Potter." Iola, Wisconsin: Krause Publications, 2000; pp.148-149.

Charlotte Foust

Aimone, Steve. *Live and Learn: Expressive Drawing*. Asheville, North Carolina: Lark Books, 2009.

Drew Galloway

Bookhardt, D. Eric. "Going With the Flow." *New Orleans Gambit*, 2001.

Feaster, Felicia. "Floating Life: Landscapes focus on lake's border zone." *Creative Loafing*, 1999.

Jones, Michelle. "Southern Alchemy." *The Tennessean*. 2009.

Jordan, Philip. "A River Finds Its Artists." *Birmingham Weekly*. 2004.

MacCash, Douglas. "Plywood Pre-Raphelites." *The Times Picyune*, 2005.

McLellan, Marion. "Hallowed Visions." *The New*

Orleans Art Review, 2004.

Rubin, Jeff. "Galloway." *The New Orleans Art Review*, 1999.

Warner, Mary Helene. "When Less Is More." *Oxford Town*. 2004.

Lilian Garcia-Roig

Baldaia, Peter. "Encounters: Lilian Garcia-Roig." Essay in Huntsville Museum of Art catalog, 2008.

Dawson, Jessica. "A 'Space' That's Filled by History's Shadow." *Washington Post*, March 27, 2009.

Flores, Tatiana. "Lilian Garcia-Roig @ Carol Jazzar Contemporary Art." *Art Nexus, Vol. 7, No. 68*, 2008; pp. 133-134.

Mills, Michael. "Time+Temp at the Art and Culture Center Proves That Painting Is Not Dead." *Broward Palm Beach Times*, December 24, 2009.

Murphy, Debra. *Arbus Magazine*, Nov. 2010; pp. 58-62.

New American Paintings: Southern editions #58, #76, #88 and 15th Anniversary edition. Boston, Massachusetts: The Open Studios Press.

"Space, Unlimited." Art Museum of the Americas Catalog, Washington, D.C.; March 2009.

Weissman, Terri. Review of "Space, Unlimited." *Art Nexus*, June 30, 2009.

Phil Garrett

"Personal Acrylic Applications." *American Artist Magazine*, December 2008; p. 15.

"Working Proof." *Art on Paper*, March/April 2002; p. 73.

Dean Gioia

"Dean Gioia." *Art Galleries & Artists of the South Magazine*, Vol. Three, Issue 2; pp. 38-39.

Gioia, Dean. "Turn of Light: The Paintings of Dean Gioia." Tallahassee, Florida: Moonrise Art, 2002.

Jeanne Goodman

Connors, Jill. "A Remodeling Story." *Country Home*, February 2007.

"Jeanne Goodman." *New American Paintings, Vol. 3*. South End, Massachusetts: Open Studios Press; April 1998.

Pyle, David. "Unleash the Potential of Colored Pencil." *Artists' Magazine*, May 1994; p. 42.

John A. Hancock

Hancock, John A. "Crucible" (Atlantic Christian College) 21, 23 (1985, 1987). Illustrations.
Loblolly 1, 2, 3, 4, (1984-1988). Illustrations.

"Merry Wives of Windsor Educational Project." Loundes County Arts Council. Illustrations. 1987.

"Watermarks: Contempoary Watermedia." Exhibition catalog, 1997.

Wilson, North Carolina: Inventory of Historical Buildings. Wilson Historical Commission, 1981.

Harrison, Helen A. "Abstraction '97." *The New York Times*, February 2, 1997.

Latter, Ruth. "Artist Deserves Credit for Reinventing Nature." *The Daily Progress*, October 9, 2003.

George Handy

500 Cups. Asheville, North Carolina: Lark Books (images and cover note), Sterling Publishing, 2006.

500 Pitchers. Asheville, North Carolina: Lark Books (images), Sterling Publishing. 2006.

Asheville: A View from the Top. Asheville, North Carolina: Roland Beers & James Turner Publishers, 1997.

Batman Forever. Artwork used in set design, Warner Bros.

Boswell, Thom. *Making and Decorating Fantastic Frames*. New York, New York: Sterling Publishing, 1993.

"Crafts in WNC – Hand-Made with Heart." *Blue Ridge Journal*, September 1993.

"George Handy: Work of the Artist." Abbey Road Productions for UNC-TV, 2001.

Hand Built Ceramics. New York, New York: Sterling Publishing, Altamont Press, 1996.

Handmade Tiles. New York, New York: Sterling Publishing, Altamont Press, 1994.

"Local Art Goes to Broadway." *Asheville Citizen-Times*, June 1992.

"Mountain Traditions." *Times News*, *New York Times*, June 2007.

"NC Artists for the 90's." *Greensboro News & Record*, January 1991.

"Tampering with Teapots." *Asheville Citizen-Times*, May 1992.

The Arts Journal. Verne Stafford. Director of Penland School. June 1985.

"The Arts of Craft." *Endless Vacation Magazine* (USAir in-flight magazine), 1992.

"The Indomitable Spirit of the Artist." *Laurel of Asheville*, November 2008.

"The Secret the Movie" (images/clips from my studio process used in filming), 2006.

Ann Harwell

500 Art Quilts. Asheville, NC: Lark Books, 2010.

Fiberarts Design Book 7. Asheville, NC: Lark Books, 2004.

Harwell, Ann. "Stories in Symmetry." *American Quilter*, Spring 2007, pp. 34-37.

Piper, Eloise. *Batik for Artists and Quilters*. Gloucester, Massachusetts: Hand Books Press, 2001.

Ed Hatch

"Capturing the luminous quality of light." *International Artist Magazine*, Aug/Sept 2009, pp. 52-59.

"Ed Hatch." *Art Galleries & Artists of the South*. Summer 2004; pp. 14-15.

"Virginia artist uses personal experience to create quietly emotive works." *American Art Collector*, December 2005, pp. 154-157.

Mana Hewitt

"Ceramics." *ART 101: Understanding Visual Artforms*. Dubuque, Iowa: Kendall/Hunt Publishing Company, 2009; Chapter 4.

Connelly, Elizabeth. "Going to Carolina." *American Style*, February 2007; p. 40.

"Constructing Copper Images." *Lake Murray Magazine*, July 2005, p. 65.

Craig, Susan. "Mukhtaran Bibi and Open Eyes, The Silent Majority" (photo). *Faith At Work*, Vol. 119, No. 3, Fall 2006; p. 7.

Day, Jeffrey. "Portrait of a Nuclear Family (photo)." *The State*, April 23, 2006; p. E1.

"Financial Figures" (photo), *The State*, 2006. pp. B1, B6.

Gilkerson, Mary. "Time, Space Key Themes in USC Faculty Exhibit." *Free Times*, January 24-30, 2007. Vol. 119, #3, p. 22.

"Hewitt, Mana. Art Beat." *Lake Murray Magazine*, March 2004.

Werner, Ben. "SC Artists adding some STYLE to new First Citizens building." *The State*, April 27, 2006.

Bill Hopen

Crosbie, Michael J. PHD, editor. "Doing more with less: Transcendent Christ, St Francis Chapel, Muncie." *Faith and Form Interfaith Journal on Religion Art and Architecture*, Vol. XLIII, No. 1, 2010. pp. 22-23.

"Meditation Before the Dance," *West Virginia Gazette*, November 19, 1995.

"Sculptor carves massive work for International Mothers Day Memorial Shrine." Susan Stamberg, interview. National Public Radio's "All Things Considered." May 12, 1982.

"Shanghai Connection Sutton-based sculptors in China: Sculptors Bill and Ai Qiu." *West*

Virginia Gazette, November 21, 2004.

"Symbol of a Senator." *West Virginia Gazette*, March 19, 1996.

Jack Hughes

Country Home and *Early American Life* (cover and featured articles), 1987-89.

Manternach, Ann Omvig. "A Bird in Hand, Jack Hughes, Carver of Wooden Decoys." *Country Home*, June 1988; pp. 110-114.

Riha, John. "An American Classic." *Country Home*, February 1989; pp. 33-48.

Geoffrey Johnson

"Art Appreciation." *Philadelphia Style Magazine*, September 2008; p. 195.

"Geoffrey Johnson: Cities of Dark & Light." *American Art Collector Magazine*, April 2007; pp. 118-123.

"On the Cover." *Poetry East Magazine*, Spring 2010; cover, p. 209.

Jennifer J L Jones

"Get Comfortable." *Better Homes and Gardens*, Sept-Oct 2003; pp. 102-108.

"Jennifer J L Jones." *FOCUS Magazine*, June-July 2006; pp. 18-19.

"Path to Understanding: The Art of Jennifer Jones." *Arbus Magazine*, Mar-Apr 2007; cover, pp. 70-75.

"The Mixed-Media Art of Jennifer J. L. Jones." *Arbus Magazine*, July-Aug 2009; cover, pp. 66-67.

Signs of the Apocalypse/ Rapture. Chicago, Illinois: Front Forty Press, 2008.

Marcus Kenney

A. D. "Picking up the Pieces." *Boston Spirit*. April/May 2005.

Byrd, C. "Marcus Kenney at Marcia Wood." *Art in America*, September 2006.

Cullem, J. "Marcus Kenney pulls out the stops." Artscriticatl.com, 2010.

"Reviews: National." ARTnews, April 2011.

Feaster, F. "Marcus Kenney." *Art Papers*, July/ Aug 2008.

Fox, C. "Savannah Artist's Stylized Stories." *The Atlanta Journal-Constitution*, December 30, 2005.

Genocchio, B. "Catching Imagination in Language and Imagery." *New York Times*, February 24, 2008.

Hansell, S. "Animals Rule." Burnaway.com, 2010.

Hersh, A. "American Icons." *Savannah Morning News*, July 1, 2007.

"Rising Star." *Savannah Magazine*, Sept/Oct 2008.

Hicks, C. "Midnight in America: Kid Nation."

Creative Loafing Atlanta, May 14, 2008.

Lew, R. "Travel: Savannah." *Southern Accents*, November/December 2007.

Lisle, A. "Kenney's Kids: Ambiguous Trios." *Commercial Appeal*, June 1, 2008.

MacCash, D. "American Undone." *New Orleans Times-Picayune*, March 9, 2007.

"Marcus Kenney." Geronimoprojects.com, 2010.

May, W. "Collage Matters." *New York Arts Magazine*, Vol. 12, No. 1 (of 2), 2007.

McQuaid, C. "On the Edge of Nostalgia." *Boston Globe*, April 22, 2005.

Moreno G. "Reviews: Boca Raton." *Art Papers*, July/Aug, 2005.

Mullarkey, M. "Myth and its Discontents." *The New York Sun*, July 7. 2005.

"New American Painting." *Southern Edition*, 2007, 2011.

Olmsted, M. "State of the Arts." *South Magazine*, February/March 2011.

Reyes, P. "Southern Artist." *Oxford American*, Fall 2005.

Young, E. "Mixed Up World of Marcus Kenney." *South Magazine*, February 2007.

Christy Kinard

"Blue Window." *Black and White* (cover), February 5-18, 1998.

Bradford-Epstein, Jennifer. "Art with Heart." *Today's Charlotte Woman*, February 2007; p.18.

Campbell, Dana Adkins. "Do the Funky Chicken." *Southern Living Magazine*, November 1999; p. 2.

Capenter, Courtney. "Four contemporary artists to add to your collection." *Southwest Art Magazine*, May 2009; pp. 38-39.

Langshore, Jane. "Exhibitionism." *Black and White*, December 4-17, 2003.

"Strange bird of childhood memories." *Piedmont Review*, Spring 1998.

"The Beverly McNeil Gallery." *Interiors and Designs of the Emerald Coast*, February-March 2002; p. 20/June-July 2003; p.47.

Clive King

Guernsey, Dan. "Interview with Clive King." *Southeastern College of Art Conference Review*, 2004.

Heller-Greenman, Bernadine. Catalog essay from Frost Art Museum, Miami, Florida, 2004.

Jones, Antony. "Painting the Dragon." National Museum of Wales, 2000.

Paine, T. Janice. "Clive-King-Weaves-His-Past-and-Present-Monumental." *Naples Daily News*, 2010.

Sale, T. and Claudia Bett. *Drawing a Contemporary Approach, 5th Edition*. Belmont, California: Wadsworth Publishing Co., 2003.

Barbara Krupp

"A Cultural Review." Middletown, New York: Sunstorm Publishing, 1985-1986.

"Focus." Brighthouse Networks, Channel 49, Melbourne, Florida; October 26, 2009.

Fugate, Marty. "Hidden Cities." *Sarasota Herald-Tribune*, 2011.

"Krupp, Barbara." *Who's Who in American Art*. New Providence, NJ: Marquis Publishing, 1990-2011.

Tracey Lane

"Best of the West: Beyond the West." *Southwest Art Magazine*, September 2008; p.45.

Campbell, Virginia. "Tales of the Trees." *Southwest Art Magazine*, February 2007; p.129.

Mowry, Lisa. "Newsworthy Neutrals: When off-duty at his Atlanta home, CNN anchor Thomas Roberts makes easygoing style the story." *Better Homes and Gardens: Decorating Magazine*, Winter 2005; p. 85.

Russell, Natalie Ermann. "Southern Accents ASID National Residential Interior Design Contest Winners." *Southern Accents Magazine*, Jan/Feb 2007; p. 41, 46.

Mernet Larsen

Bennett, Lennie. "All the Corners of her World: Inside the Singular Mind of Painter Mernet Larsen." *St. Petersburg Times*, May 2, 2010.

Cohen, David. "The Fitting Room." Catalog essay: Vogt Gallery, New York, 2011.

Feaster, Filicia. "Review: Marcia Wood Gallery, Atlanta." *Art Papers*, May/June 2011; p. 40.

Naves, Mario. "Mernet Larsen's Tilting Panoramas: Methodical and Inspired Work." *The New York Observer*, January 31, 2005.

Schwartz, Joyce. "Transitory Patterns." Catalog essay: National Museum of Women in the Arts, 2004.

Ruth Laxon

"A Hundred Years of: LEX FLEX" (review), *Art on Paper*, 2003.

"Artist Survival Page and Review Retell the Tale." *Art Papers*, 1997.

Bright, Betty. "(HO plus GO)2+IT in Art's Fragile Vehicle." *Art Papers*, 1990.

Byrd, Cathy. "Review Ruth Laxson at Maria Wood." *Art in America*, 2003.

"Review, Point of View." *Creative Loafing*, 2002.

Cullum, Jerry. "After Thoughts." *Atlanta Constitution*, 1997.

"Drawn in GA." *Atlanta Journal-Constitution*, 2006.

"Review Retell the Tale." *Art Papers*, 1998.

Drucker, Johanna. "Review Muse Measures." *Livres D'Artistes*, 2000.

The Century of Artists. New York, New York: Granary Books, 1995.

"Cover Design: Feature on A Hundred Years of: LEX FLEX." *Journal of Artist's Books #20*, 2003.

Finkelstein, David. "Review." *Art Papers*, 1987.

Fox, Catherine. "Books give 'unique voice' room to play." *Atlanta Journal-Constitution*, 2005.

"Profile," *Atlanta Constitution*, 1997.

"Review of Read the Mail." *Atlanta Constitution*, 1993.

"Word Art: Laxson Melds" (text and image), *Atlanta Journal-Constitution*, 2002.

Harper, Glen. "Some Things are Sacred." *Afterimage*, 1991.

Hastings, P. B. "Fall Feature Interview." *Journal of Artistic Books*, 1997.

Higgins, Dick. "Measure – Cut – Stitch, review." *Art Papers*, 1988.

Hoffberg, Judith. "11 by 11, Lit. Tyrannies." *Umbrella*, 1991.

"Review Letters to the Ether/Other." *Umbrella*, 1997.

"Review of Muse Measures." *Umbrella*, 1999.

"Summer Review – Measure – Cut – Stitch." *High Performance*, 1988.

Hubert, Renee. *The Cutting Edge of Reading Artists' Books*. New York, New York: Granary Books, 1999.

Medina, Angel. "June Review: After Thoughts." *Art Papers*, 1997.

"Photos of RETELL THE TALE and LEX FLEX." *The Penland Book of Hand-Made Paper*. Asheville, North Carolina: Lark Books, 2004.

Princenthal, Nancy. "Measure – Cut – Stitch." *Print Collector's News*, 1988.

"Review Muse Measures." *Art on Paper*, 2000.

Warren Smith, Virginia. "Interview." *Art Papers*, 1992.

Peter Lenzo

500 Figures in Clay: Ceramic Artists Celebrate the Human Form. Asheville, North Carolina: Lark Books, 2004.

Hunter, Robert, ed. *Ceramics in America*. Milwaukee, Wisconsin: Chipstone Foundation, 2006.

Poetic Expressions of Mortality: Figurative Ceramics from the Porter-Price Collection. Mobile, Alabama: Mobile Museum of Art, 2006.

Roefs, Wim. "Construction Crew: Klaus Hartmann, Kim Keats, Peter Lenzo & Edward Rice." Columbia, SC: if ART, International Fine Art Services, 2005.

Robert Levin

500 Glass Objects. Asheville, NC: Lark Books, 2006.

Leier, Ray, Jan Peters, and Kevin Wallace. *Contemporary Glass - Color, Light and Form*. Madison, Wisconsin: Guild Publishing, 2001.

"Robert Levin." *Craft Arts International (Australia)*, Issue 59, 2003.

Who's Who in American Art. Berkeley Heights, New Jersey: Marquis Publishing, 2010.

Alan Loehle

Abernathy, Jeremy. "Raw Materials; Dissecting the Works of Alan Loehle." *Art Voices*, January 2009; p. 16.

Feaster, Felicia. "The Beastmaster." *The Atlantan*, January/February 2009; p. 36.

Fox, Catherine. "Exploring Old and New Themes." *The Atlanta Journal Constitution*, January 23, 2009; p. E7.

"Portfolio: Six Dogs." *The Paris Review*, #148, Fall 1998; pp. 99-105.

Lindsey Mears

500 Handmade Books: Inspiring Interpretations of a Timeless Form. Asheville, North Carolina: Lark Books, 2008.

Littleton, Maurine. *500 Glass Objects: A Celebration of Functional & Sculptural Objects*. Asheville, North Carolina: Lark Books, 2006.

"Not Exactly by the Book." *American Style Magazine*, Summer 2003.

Tjelda vander Meijden

Art in Embassies Program. "United States Embassy Reykjavik." Published by AIEP, November 2003.

Collins, Bradford R. Ph.D, and Ellen Dressler. *Contemporary Charleston 2004*. Charleston, South Carolina: City of Charleston Cultural Affairs, May 2004.

Villani, John. "The Creative Tourist." *The Santa Fe New Mexican*, June 6, 1999.

Luisa Mesa

Hargot, Angie. "The Work Line: Luisa Mesa Draws on Experience to Analyze an Art Consciousness." *The Lead*, April 30, 2010: pp. 10-11.

Langston, Angel. "Local artist completes work at 2020 Ponce Office Tower." Communitynewspapers.com, September 7-13, 2010; p. 12.

Moreno, Sara. "Tres Perspectivas del Paisaje Interior." *El Nuevo Herald*, October 15 2007; p. E1.

Suarez de Jesus, Carlos. "Spinning Right 'Round." *Miami New Times*, June 8-14, 2006; p. 33.

Tischler, Gary. "Redefining Boundaries: IDB Shows There's More to Miami Than Sun and Fun." *The Washington Diplomat*, April 2008; p. 41.

Philip Morsberger

Gruber, J. Richard, ed. *Philip Morsberger: Paintings and Drawings from the Sixties*. Augusta, Georgia: Morris Museum of Art, 2000.

Landauer, Susan, ed. *The Lighter Side of Bay Area Figuration*. Kansas City, Missouri: Kemper Museum of Contemporary Art, 2000.

Lloyd, Christoper. *Philip Morsberger: A Passion for Painting*. London/New York: Merrell Publishers Ltd., 2007.

Tanner, Marcia. *Philip Morsberger*. San Francisco, California: Rena Bransten Gallery, 1990.

Dorothy Netherland

"Artist Dorothy Netherland Paints a New Reality." *Charleston City Paper*, February 1, 2011.

"Contemporary Charleston 2009: Revelation of Process." Exhibition catalog and DVD, 2009.

"Dorothy Netherland Interview." meryltruett. com, 2010.

"Revelation of Process Compiles Eclectic Talent for Piccolo." *The Post and Courier*, May 21, 2009.

Keith Norval

Elam, Shade. "Making Room For Art." *The News and Observer*, June 17, 2007.

Norval, Keith. "Self Service." *Lather Weekly*, Jan. 2003.

Marcelo Novo

Diggs, Peggy, Laura Steward Heon and JosephThompson. *Billboard: Art On The Road, Mass.* Museum of Contemporary Art, North Adams, MA, 1999 (co-published with MIT Press, Cambridge, MA).

Hartvigsen, Kristine. "Engaging the Muse." *Lake Murray-Columbia Magazine*, May 2008; pp. 46-47.

King, Aaron. "Meet The NoVA Newcomers." *Northern Virginia Magazine*, January 2011; p. 51.

Tynes, Teri. "The Rise of Marcelo Novo." *Free Times*, May 10, 2000; cover and pp. 26-27.

Barbara Olsen

Chassman, G. M. *In The Spirit of Martin*. Atlanta, Georgia: Tinwood Books, Verve Edition 2001; p. 128, 205, 218.

Christian, Barbara. "Folk Artist is Story Teller in a Painter's Smock." *Chagrin Falls Times*, December 29, 1994; pp. B1-B3.

Foley, Jill. "Brushing Up On History." *Country Home*, October 1997; pp. 110-119.

Guettinger, Roger. "Modern Americana, The Naive Imagery of Barbara Olsen." *American Club, Hong Kong Town & Country News*, October 1989; pp. 18, 19.

Hagan, Debbie. "Art in the 2nd Dimension." *Niche Magazine*, Winter 2001, pp. 75-81/ Spring 2001, pp. 80-83.

Irwin, Anne. "Anne Irwin Fine Art." Atlanta, GA, 2009.

Sanrio, Fukugo Vision Institute. "Barbara Olsen." *Exit Magazine Tokyo, Japan*, December 1991; 2 pg.

Williams, Suzanne and Barbara Olsen. *The Witch Casts a Spell*. New York, New York: Dial Books, Penguin Putnam, 2002.

Janet Orselli

Day, Jeffrey. "Battered Beauty." *The State*, March 20, 2000; E1-2.

O'Sullivan, Joanne. "A Life Less Ordinary." *Bold Life*, October 2009; pp. 30-32.

Tynes, Teri. "Reviews (Southeast): Triennial 2001." *Art Paper*, Nov/Dec. 2001; pp. 66-67.

Matt Overend

"Colorful Art Fills The Air At Moonshell Gallery." *The Island Packet*. Hilton Head, South Carolina, May 28, 2004.

"Less Is More To S.C. Painter." *Charlotte (NC) Observer*, January 9, 2004; p. 18E.

Roefs, Wim. "Construction Crew II: Matt Overend, Virginia Scotchie, Christine Tedesco & Paul Yanko." if ART, International Fine Art Services, 2006.

"Double 0 80808: Janet Orselli & Matt Overend." Columbia, South Carolina: if ART, International Fine Art Services, 2005.

Jan Clayton Pagratis

"The Art in Embassies Program," Ambassador Charles P. Reis, Athens Greece, The U.S. Department of State, Washington D.C., October 2005.

Adams, Laura. "East End Gallery." *Connect*, October 6-12, 2000; p. 82.

Dawers, Bill. "Grass-roots art shows rally." *Savannah Morning News*, May 8, 2008; p. 9E.

Hersh, Allison. "European Landscapes." *Savannah Morning News*, August 4, 2002; p. 12E and 14E.

"Reduce, Reuse, Recycle." *Savannah Morning News*, May 11, 2008; p. 4E.

Kontaraki, Despina. "Art is a Global Language." *Apogevmatini*, January 27, 2006.

Martin, Robert and Jean Alsopp. "Outdoor Porch." *Southern Living Magazine*, September 2003; cover and p. 84.

Nazdin, Joany. "Multiplicity." Southern Maryland Newspapers Online (www.somdnews.com), October 28, 2008.

Rutherford, Tim. "The Long & Winding Road." *Coastal Antiques and Art*, December 2000; p. 4.

"Five Artists to Collect." *Coastal Antiques and Art*, January 2003; Vol. 8. No. 5, p 10-11.

Roger Palmer

Cullum, Jerry. "Review of solo show at Marcia Wood." *Atlanta Journal-Constitutions*, September 2008.

Norr, David. "In Dog Light." Catalog essay, solo show, University of South Florida Contemporary Art Museum, 2008.

Voeller, Megan. "Roger Palmer Lets the Dogs Out." *Creative Loafing*, Tampa, Florida, July 16, 2008.

Tere Pastoriza

Garcia, Vanessa. "At Mid-life a Painter Comes Into Her Own." *Neighbors Section: The Miami Herald*, January 12, 2006; p. 8.

Herrera, Adriana. "Rutas del Arte." *El Nuevo Herald*, January 10, 2006; p. D1.

John Douglas Powers

Adams, Cynthia. "John Powers: Visual Echoes Invoke His Art." *University of GA Graduate School Magazine*, Winter 2009.

Bostick, Alan. "Power Mechanics." *The Tennessean*, December 22, 2002.

Buchanan, Charles. "UAB Professor of Sculpture John Powers Assembles 'Remember'." UAB News Blazercast, December 23, 2008.

Dallow, Jessica. "Time Spent, an Interview with John Douglas Powers." *The SECAC Review*, Vol. XLI, No. 5.

Fox, Cathy. "Sprawling Sculpture Feast Exudes Grass-Roots Charm." *Atlanta Journal-Constitution*, January 28.

Jones, MiChelle. "John Douglas Powers' Kinetic Sculpture Taps Into Memories." *The Tennessean*, Jan. 18, 2009.

"Simple Complexity," *The Tennessean*, November 29, 2009.

Kaczmarczyk. Jeffrey. "Meet the Artists, Here's a Look at ArtPrize's Top 10 Creators." *Grand Rapids Press*, October 4, 2009.

Maynard, Michelle. "Eyes on the Art Prize," *New York Times*, October 8, 2009.

Nelson, James. "John Powers' Mechanical Sculptures are Hypnotic," *The Birmingham News*, July 25, 2010.

"Powers' Work Stirs Like Wheat In A Breeze," *The Birmingham News*, February 14, 2010.

Nolan, Joe. "Simple Complexity," *The Nashville Scene*, December 3, 2009.

"Rebooting the Conversation." WGVU-TV, Nov. 25, 2009, Grand Rapids, MI. Art Prize documentary directed by Patrick Center and produced by Jim Vander Maas.

Richett, Emily. "Art Prize Top 10: Field of Reeds." FOX 17 News, October 6, 2009.

Whitley, Carla Jean. "John Douglas Powers: Myths, culture, and life experiences create meaning in this artist's kinetic sculptures." *Birmingham Magazine*, January 2010: Vol. 50, No. 1.

Susie Pryor

1999-2009: Included in various articles in *Art Galleries and Artists of the South*, *Atlanta Homes and Lifestyles*, *Atlanta Style and Design*, and other magazines.

Paul Reed

Haynie, Ron. "Paul Reed: Paintings, Sculptures, Photographs, Prints 1961-1996." Washington, D.C.: Watkins Gallery, American University.

Humblet, Claudine. *The New American Abstraction 1950-1970, 2nd Volume*. Milan, Italy: Skira Editore S.p.A., 2007.

McClintic, Miranda. *Modernism & Abstraction: Treasures from the Smithsonian American Art Museum*. Washington, D.C.: Smithsonian American Art Museum, 2001.

Roefs, Wim. "Abstract in Nature: Paul Reed, Laura Spong, Katie Walker and Mike Williams." Columbia, South Carolina: if ART Gallery, 2007.

Edward Rice

Grogan, Kevin. *Preservation of Place: The Art of Edward Rice*. Augusta, Georgia: Morris Museum of Art, 2011.

Gruber, J. Richard and David Houston. *The Art of the South: 1890-2003*. New Orleans,

Louisiana/London, England: Ogden Museum of Art/Scala Publishers, 2004.

Houston, David, ed. *Edward Rice: Architectural Works 1978-1998*. Augusta, Georgia: The Gertrude Herbert Institute of Art. 1998.

Roefs, Wim. "Edward Rice: Paintings 1996-2008." Columbia, South Carolina: if ART Gallery, 2007.

Barbara Rivera

Dimitrescu, Marta. "Art Now 2005, online Global Art Annual." Artoteque.com, 2005.

Goldberb Longstreth, Peg. "A Must-See at the 'Florida Contemporary'." *Naples Florida Weekly*, 2010.

Herrera, Adriana. "Young Talent en el Miami Design District." *El Nuevo Herald*, 2004.

Russu, Petru. "Barbara Rivera." *Famous 120 Contemporary Artists*. World of Art books, 2007.

Mark Rutkowski

Rutkowski, Mark. *South Beach, Two Decades of Deco District Paintings*. Atglen, PA: Schiffer Publishing, 2006.

Mary Ann Scherr

Diamonstein, Barbara. *Handmade in America: Conversations with Fourteen Craftmasters*. New York, New York: Harry N. Abrams Inc. 1995.

Dictionary of International Biography du BIJOU. London, United Kingdom: Melrose Press, 1998.

Grant-Lewin, Susan. *One of a Kind: American Art Jewel Today*. New York, New York: Harry N. Abrams, 1994.

Kirkham, Pat. *Women Designers in the USA: Diversity and Difference 1900-2000*. New Haven, Connecticut: Yale University Press, 2001.

Lamarre, Rachel. *Grand Prix Des Metiers D'Art*. Montreal, Canada: privately published, 1996.

L'Ecuyer, Kelly H. *Jewelry By The Artists: In the Studio 1942-2000*. Boston, Massachusetts: MFA Publications, 2010.

LeVan, Martha. *The Penland Book of Jewelry*. New York, New York: Lark Books/Sterling Publishing, Inc., 2005.

McCreught. *Metal Technic*. Cape Elizabeth, Maine: Bynmorgan Press, 1992.

McGrath, Jinks. *The Encyclopedia of Jewelry Technique*. London, United Kingdom: Quarto Publishing, 1995.

Metcalf, Bruce and Janet KoPlos. *A History of America Studio Craft*. Chapel Hill, North Carolina: University of North Carolina Press, 2010.

Sothaby's. *The Andy Warhol Collection*. New York, New York: Harry N. Abrams, 1998.

Untracht, Oppi. *Jewelry Concepts and Technology*. New York, New York: Doubleday, 1982.

Watkins, David. *Design Sourcebook: Jewelry*. London, United Kingdom: New Holland Pub Ltd., 1999.

Kim Schuessler

1998-2009: Included in various articles in *Better Homes and Gardens*, *Atlanta Magazine*, *Florida Design*, *Palm Beach Illustrated*, and other magazines.

Davis, Stephanie. "Mothers and Daughters," *Skirt Magazine*, 2009; p. 32.

"Kim Schuessler, Amy Cole and Christy Kinard." *Art Galleries & Artists of the South*. August-October 2003; p. 34-35.

Mayer, Caitlin. "Kim Schuessler." *Pink Magazine*, April 2011; cover and p. 9.

Overcash, Anita. "Group Hug: New Works by Geoffrey Johnson and Kim Schuessler." *Creative Loafing*, May 2009.

Virginia Scotchie

"Australian Ceramics Triennal," *The Journal of Australian Ceramics*, p. 20-22.

Brown, Glenn R. "The Familiar in Art and Object," *Ceramics Monthly*, May 2005; cover and pp. 28-32.

"Objects Near and Far," *Ceramics Monthly*, February 2010; p. 24.

UNDEFINED Magazine (cover, feature).

Ebeth Scott-Sinclair

Greenberg, Blue. "Shows are Art Lovers Delight." *The Herald-Sun*, July 13, 2008.

Nelson, James R. "Paintings Have Level of Ruefulness; Kinard Works Utterly Charming." *The Birmingham News*, May 13, 2007.

"Recent Works by Ebeth Scott-Sinclair." *The Birmingham News*, March 15, 2009.

Thomas Jerry Siegel

Siegel, Jerry. *FACING SOUTH, Portraits of Southern Artists*. Tuscaloosa, AL: University of Alabama Press, 2011.

Laura Spong

Roefs, Wim. "Abstracted in Nature: Reiner Mählein, Silvia Rudolf & Laura Spong." Columbia, South Carolina: if ART Gallery, 2008.

"Laura Spong at 80: Warming the Chill Wind with Celebration." Columbia, South Carolina: if ART, International Fine Art Services, 2006.

"Laura Spong 2006-2011: Age As an Administrative Device." Columbia, SC: if

ART Gallery, 2011.

"Laura Spong: The Early Works." Columbia, South Carolina: if ART Gallery, 2007.

Katherine Taylor

Cullum, Jerry. "Artists Question Southern Art?" GA State's Welch Gallery: Burnaway Org., July 20, 2010.

Fox, Catherine. "Silent Images Bear Witness to Cataclysm." *The Atlantic Journal-Constitution*, October 15, 2010.

Kurzner, Lisa. *Atlanta, Homes and Lifestyles*, September 2007; pp. 70-71.

Richmond, Susan. *Art Papers*, May/June 2009; p. 48.

W. Gerome Temple

Cullum, Jerry. "OUTSIDE THE LINES: Imaginary world, richly detailed." *Atlanta Journal Constitution*, March 2008.

Hersh, Allison. "Fantasy Worlds." *Savannah Morning News*, February 2004.

"Part Art, Part Drafting, Sprinkled with a Dose of Art History." *Coastal Arts and Antiques*, February 2003.

Talor, Christina. "Circus Scenes with a Delicate Air." *The GA Guardian*, February 1999.

Dayna Thacker

Abernathy, Jeremy. Review. *Art Papers*, Sept/Oct 2010.

Fox, Catherine. "Where unknowns, pros share space," *The Atlanta Journal-Constitution*, May 27, 2011; p. D5.

New American Paintings, #82 Southern Edition, 2009

Wyatt Williams "Art Seen: Dayna Thacker at Barbara Archer." *Creative Loafing*, June 17, 2010.

Claudia Gibson Thomas

"Winter Garden in Plein Air opening Mar 13." *West Orange Times*, 2009; Social Section.

Matt Toole

Bates, Mary. "Third International Conference on Contemporary Cast Iron Art" (photograph). *Sculpture*, 1998.

Centro Cultural Paraguayo Americano, "3rd Bi-National Art Exhibit," 2003.

Doran, John. "Firing the Imagination." *Artwork*, No. 100, 1999.

Forbes, J. B. "Artist Strives for Creation Through Destruction." *St. Louis Post-Dispatch*, 2000.

Fremantle, Chris. "Iron Conference: The Art of Recidivism?" chris.fremantle.org/2010/07/; 2010.

Grant, Ashley H. "Sculpture Park Artists Think Big- Really Big." *The Oregonian*, 2002.

Hersh, Alison. "Poetry in Motion." *The Savannah Morning News*, 2008.

Holley, Mary Ann. "Sculpture Becomes the Performer in Matt Toole's Arts/Industry Project." *The Sheboygan Press*, 2001.

Husband, Bertha. "Matt Toole's 'Kinetic." *Connect Savannah*, 2008.

Maddox, Teri. "Sculpting with Fire." *Belleville News-Democrat*, 2000.

Whitney, Kathleen. "Iron Tribe." *World Sculpture News*, 2001.

Leo Twiggs

Campbell, Mary Schmidt, and Elton C. Fax. *Leo Twiggs: Downhome Landscapes – Batik Paintings*. New York, New York: The Studio Museum in Harlem, 1978.

Laufer, Marilyn, ed. *Myths and Metaphors: The Art of Leo Twiggs*. Athens, Georgia: GA Museum of Art, 2004.

Twiggs, Leo. *Messages from Home: The Art of Leo Twiggs*. Orangeburg, South Carolina: Claflin University Press, 2011.

Roefs, Wim. *Leo Twiggs: Toward Another Retrospective*. Columbia, South Carolina: if ART, International Fine Art Services, 2006.

Mary Walker

Katz, Lynn Barstis Williams. *Reconsidering Regionalism: Prints Inspired by the South, 1951-2011*. Auburn, Alabama: Auburn University, 2011.

Rhodes, Kristen. "Creative Process." *Charleston Magazine*, March 2009; p. 62.

Smith, Nick. "Text Messages." *City Paper*, January 10, 2007; p. 43.

"Must-See Scrolls." *City Paper*, Nov. 2005; p. 29F.

Kathleen Westkaemper

Kathleen Westkaemper, Featured Artist, Dott Art Gallery, August 2010. (http://www.dottartgallery.com/index_files/Page309.html).

Enid Williams

Hicks, Ann. "Artists Take Bold Stroke with 7 x 7." Review. *Greenville News*, 2007.

Rudolph, Ellen. "Enid Williams and Paul Yanko: Paintings from A Marriage." *Angle Magazine*, Vol. 2, No. 22, Sept/Oct 2005; pp. 11-12.

Woody, Michael. "If These Walls Could Talk" (interview). *Deep Magazine*, September 2007.

Mike Williams

"Daniel Wallace." *Garden and Gun Magazine*. March/April 2008; pp. 80-87.

"Janna McMahan." *South Carolina Wildlife*, Mar/Apr 1999; pp. 24-35.

Madden, Ed. *Signals: Poems* (front cover art). Columbia, South Carolina: The University of South Carolina Press, 2008.

Roefs, Wim. *Up From the Mud - Aaron Baldwin and Mike Williams*. Columbia, South Carolina: if Art, International Fine Art Services, 2005.

David H. Yaghjian

"Coming Back Home." *The State*, September 24, 2000; pp. F1-2.

"One Time in the South." *Atlanta Journal Constitution*, July 11, 1997; p. 10.

Roefs, Wim, ed. *David Yaghjian: Everyman Turns Six*. Columbia, South Carolina: if ART Gallery, 2011.

"Studio Visits." *At the Museum*. Greenville, South Carolina: Greenville County Museum of Art, June 2007; pp. 2-3.

Paul Yanko

Roefs, Wim. "Construction Crew II." Catalog essay. Columbia, South Carolina: if ART Gallery, 2006.

Rudolph, Ellen. "Enid Williams and Paul Yanko: Paintings from A Marriage." *Angle Magazine*, Vol. 2, No. 22, September/October 2005; pp. 11-12.

Utter, Douglas Max. "Dancing the Orange" (catalog essay). Youngstown, Ohio: McDonough Museum of Art, 2002.

Index